The Goodness *of* Ordinary People

The
Goodness
of
Ordinary
People

TRUE STORIES FROM REAL AMERICANS

Faith Middleton

CROWN PUBLISHERS, INC. ❧ NEW YORK

NOTE: If a caller's name was not given, I have assigned one. Any minor adjustments in their testimony were made only to preserve clarity or meaning.

Published by Crown Publishers, Inc., 201 East 50th Street, New York, New York 10022. Member of the Crown Publishing Group.

Random House, Inc.   New York, Toronto, London, Sydney, Auckland

CROWN is a trademark of Crown Publishers, Inc.

Printed in the United States of America

Design by Barbara Balch

Library of Congress Cataloging-in-Publication available upon request

ISBN: 0-517-79963-4

10   9   8   7   6   5   4   3   2   1

First Edition

for Blanche

ACKNOWLEDGMENTS

For fifteen years, two people have been brilliant and un-selfish in their contributions to my life and work. Bruce Clements suggested some of the best questions that were asked on my show, and he is a substantial presence in this book. Dr. Nancy Horn mentored me in valuing the goodness of ordinary people, while convincing me that being a bad girl also has its charms. Nancy's insight—that acknowledging goodness makes us want to become even better than we are—is the kernel from which this book grew.

I am most grateful for my friends.

I thank my Connecticut Public Television and Radio colleagues, especially President Jerry Franklin; directors John Berky, Larry Rifkin, Donna Collins, Sharon Blair, Alfred Steele, Jay Whitsett, Steve Futternich, Anita Ford-Saunders, and Cynthia Dul; and former vice president Midge Ramsey.

My editor at Crown, Betty A. Prashker, provided the freedom and guidance that enabled me to complete this project. Without her interest, the words of the people on these pages would have continued to vanish into air. Assistant Editor Dakila Divina was terrific. Publicist Penny Simon and staff were outstanding. My agent, Esther Newberg, and lawyer, Mike Rudell, were superb, as was copy editor Maureen Clark.

I don't know how to thank Gina Barreca, author of

Sweet Revenge, for her special friendship and unfailing generosity and wit, and Roxanne Coady of R. J. Julia Booksellers, who, along with Henry Berliner of The Foundry, continuously remind me of how wonderful independent bookstores are.

Although many others deserve to be named here, special thanks must go to the Community Foundation of Greater New Haven; producers Diane Orson, Bill Storandt, and Rex Cadwallader; Leah Berliner, Edward Bennett, readers Betsy Johnson, Stacey D'Erasmo, Suzanne Pinto, Gina Barreca, Meryl Cohn, Peter Perl; Michelle Bozzuto, Michael Meyer, the Chauvin family, Molly Helms, K. C. Sulotz, Jill and Kevin Aspinwall of Hamilton Communications for all those cassettes; the Vlock-Arbonies family, Penny Bellamy and Remy Zimmerman; Charlayne Hunter-Gault, for her memoir and Gail Godwin quote; and a true inspiration, Charles Kuralt.

To my family, Sally, Bruce, Jim, Barbara, Judy, Suzanne, Doug, Jane, Dan, Margaret, Danny, Megan, Jeannie, Roger, Rose Ann, Sharon, Sarah, Tommy, Dawn, Scott, and Robin, I will always love you.

When I struggled in writing this book to say what I meant, when I needed a friend, I had the best sounding board and writing coach anyone could have—Blanche McCrary Boyd.

For my sister Sally, this promise—that I will be there to love and take care of you. This book is also yours.

I am not an optimist,
because I am not sure that everything ends well.
Nor am I a pessimist,
because I am not sure that everything ends badly.
I just carry hope in my heart.

—Václav Havel

The Goodness *of* Ordinary People

Introduction

A journalist with an interest in goodness can get a bad reputation. Think about it: Clark Kent was a wimp. Still, I have spent much of my career focusing on individual and community achievement wherever I happen to discover it.

On my daily Connecticut Public Radio show, I often ask unusual questions of people calling in, and I find I have an underreported story on my hands—about the goodness of ordinary people.

I didn't set out to explore this material, but it became increasingly compelling to hear the answers to questions that have included: What would your life look like if you were guaranteed not to fail? What is it that no one can take away from you? What teacher will you always remember? What lie are you glad you told? Who believed in you at a critical time? Who have you stood up for? What would you like your tombstone epitaph to say? (The responses to this one were hilarious.)

In answering these kinds of questions, listeners tell

nourishing and extraordinary stories about themselves and others. That is what this book is all about. I regularly hear from people who see a challenge and try to meet it; who stick up for others when they need it; who are committed to trying to be fair, courageous, compassionate, generous, constant, open to the grace of forgiveness; and, perhaps hardest of all, who try to understand those who are different from themselves. These listeners demonstrate the breadth of creative and spiritual ingenuity commonly present in secular life.

I offer this document of stories in the hope that it will do for others what it has done for me. When I feel drained by the drumbeat of negativity, violence, and cynicism in so much media coverage, I think of the stories presented here and find that I am energized, delighted, and touched.

We live in a world where only the negative is considered news, and this often prevents us from seeing the tremendous strength of character in our midst.

The idea that reporting on goodness is somehow saccharine or corny cuts us off not only from the deeper currents of life but from simple accuracy. Of course terrible things happen, but to strip these things away from a larger context is both numbing and false. People who want to throw away their television sets are not rejecting the news, they are rejecting the *dishonesty* of the news. Besides, it's silly to talk about goodness as corny when it is, in fact, a heroic response to suffering.

I agree with Tobias Wolff, who says, in the introduction for *The Vintage Book of Contemporary American Short Stories,* "I have never been able to understand the complaint that a story is 'depressing' because of its subject matter. What depresses me are the stories that don't seem to know these things go on, or hide them in resolute chipperness . . . please. We're grownups now, we get to stay in the kitchen when the other grownups talk."

But just as turning our backs on what is wrong is unrealistic, an exclusive media focus on conflict, the habit of drawing attention to stories by pitting one idea or person against another, regardless of subject matter, is too limiting. It was my own longing for something more reflective of the richness of our humanity that sent me in a different direction. I have had faith that if I talk up to people, many will respond in kind.

Carpenters, CEOs, truck drivers, artists, cops, teachers, academics, and homemakers have phoned in to talk from their hearts. They are an important—and interesting—part of the story of who we are.

2

*T*he fresh orange juice was poured and my buttered raisin bagel was still hot, when I opened the *New York Times,* and nearly choked on the headline OPTIMISM AND CHEERFULNESS PREDICT A SHORTER LIFE. The story said that a team of researchers had tracked a group of optimistic people, who died sooner than unhappy people.

Assuming the worst about most situations is not an

unfamiliar concept to me. That was the unspoken rule when I was learning to be a reporter twenty-five years ago. I like to joke with my reporter friends that Milton is the patron saint of journalism because he convinced us that Satan is a lot more interesting than God.

I became a reporter by accident. In 1968, when the country was in the midst of a social revolution, I took a job as "Women's Editor" at the *Willimantic Chronicle,* a small daily newspaper in Connecticut, to help pay my way through college. I had never been inside a newspaper building before, and if I hadn't decided to interview the longtime United Nations radio correspondent Pauline Frederick, I wouldn't have realized that only a decade earlier women were not allowed in newsrooms at all. I sat there wide-eyed, as Pauline described her working conditions at NBC. She would have to stand in the newsroom door until a copyboy raced over, took her story, and carried it to an editor across the floor. Whether their hands could touch I have no idea. I recalled her story a few years later, when my newspaper ran a large front-page picture of the women at our paper sitting together with a bartender: Connecticut had just passed a law allowing women to actually sit at a bar.

At small newspapers, reporters are asked to learn everything, which is wonderful training. Mirroring the big debate on the streets of America about women, men, and social convention, I wrote about weddings, births, and deaths one minute, and covered crime and education the next. I sometimes took pictures to accompany my stories.

I had to go toe-to-toe with editors who thought a woman couldn't handle a night accident scene.

I was hooked by journalism immediately. I met interesting people all the time. I was paid to study a subject and report what I learned. It was exciting, powerful, and always amazing when I walked to the corner deli for a sandwich and the guy on the stool was reading my story.

In the early years, I worked full-time or freelance as an editor and reporter for a variety of local and national newspapers and magazines. How could radio be anything but superficial compared to what I did, I secretly thought; after all, the words were there and then they disappeared.

But when public radio began across the country, the art of radio in America seemed to change. There was more time to tell stories in interesting ways. I heard not just words and music but the sounds of waterfalls, wind, rain, laughter, ambulances, babies being born, people talking on street corners. And all these sounds were real, not manufactured in a studio.

Fifteen years ago, when I was asked to begin my prime-time show from the New Haven studios, I agreed to try it for fun. I have been at it day after day ever since. I've gone after crooks, exposed consumer rip-offs, and satirized some holy institutions, but the truth is that what interests me most is finding ways to help people understand one another. It's not a bad calling.

CHAPTER ONE

The Goodness of Ordinary People

I love what I do. I sit in a big, comfortable wing chair, usually with a cup of something hot and delicious on the side table next to me, and the calls come rolling in, one after another.

I remember the afternoon that Kate phoned me. I had just picked up my mug of Lemon Zinger tea when I heard her say her name, strong and clear. I guessed she was in her early forties. I imagine and sense all kinds of things about callers by the sounds of their voices, just as I'm sure they do about me. Kate was responding to the question that day, what was your most memorable encounter with a stranger?

Her encounter occurred when she was married to an artist and living a simple life in northern Iowa. Kate's husband had his heart set on entering his work in an art show in Florida, but the couple could not afford the cost of shipping his giant canvases across the country. Kate volunteered to strap the paintings to the roof of their old Volkswagen and drive them to the show.

"I was making this long trip by myself, going through the Smoky Mountains, and suddenly there on the side of the road stood a young boy holding a guitar and small backpack." Perhaps sensing my wariness, Kate tried to reassure me that stopping was no idle decision. "I'd been taught since childhood never to pick up strangers, but there was something about this kid. . . . I pulled over, backed up the VW, and the boy got in. After only a few miles he began to open up, telling me that he was four-teen years old and that he'd been busted for smoking marijuana by his dad, a policeman. He had run away from home and had been gone eighteen months."

Kate decided to strike a bargain with her passenger, proposing that she would take him with her to Florida if he would call his dad when they arrived. Devouring the fried chicken she bought for him, the boy mumbled something about having only sixteen cents left.

"I asked him what he would have done if I hadn't picked him up and he said quietly, 'I thought I'd wait three more cars, and if no one picked me up I would jump.'

"And that made up my mind to take him with me all the way to Florida. He did call his dad when we got there, and he sent him the money to come home by bus. About four months later I got a letter from the boy, who said he had a new baby sister, and he was going to try to make something of himself. It was just one of those in-spired moments in my life."

When Kate was through, I was confirmed in my belief that while my profession knows how to report obvious acts of heroism that occur during natural disasters, like hurricanes, when it comes to stories like Kate's, we rarely hear them. Common goodness is our vast, unreported story.

THE WAYS WE STAY CLOSE

*A*ir poetry is how I describe the moments when a caller says something that seems to hang in the air and shimmer. It happened on the day that we celebrated fathers. My guest, former *New York Times* reporter Andrew Malcolm, had written a book about how football had brought him closer to his children. He seemed surprised when I asked him to join me for a call-in show, not about the joys of football, but about what I see as the secret traditions some fathers have with their children to stay close.

Christine's story was brief. "When my father died thirty-eight years ago, we were not terribly close. He was a remote man who found it difficult to express his emotions. But we had one tradition that I will always remember because it taught me a lot about overcoming fear. Something about the power of thunderstorms attracted him. Whenever there was a thunderstorm, he'd throw open the screen and stand at the window with his elbows on the windowsill and just watch. I was very excited one day when he sort of invited me to stand with him. As time went on, watching the storm and the beautiful lightning, we kind of moved a little closer to each other until our elbows were touching. We'd just stand there and watch the storm, not saying anything, and I think it was the only closeness we ever really had. To this day, whenever there's a thunderstorm, I stand in the window."

GOOD STORYTELLING

Many strangers are memorable, if you offer them a chance to be. The key is giving people the room to surprise you.

When a man named Michael phoned, I recognized immediately from the crackle on the line that he was calling from his car. I regularly ask car-phone callers to describe what they see around them on the road, but in Michael's case, I snapped to attention because of the resonance and intensity he projected. "I just had a flashback to the first time I experienced stark terror through music. When I was just eleven years old, I was in London with my grandmother for my very first opera performance and, obviously, I was dragged there kicking and screaming. But I recall sitting there for a while and feeling really good about what I was seeing. At the end of the first act, Maria Callas plunged a dagger into Tito Gobbi's chest and the scream he gave produced such a feeling of incredible terror that people were screaming and fainting in their seats. And then Callas moved his dead body into the form of a crucifix, with candelabra on each side of him, as the curtain slowly came down for intermission. My grandmother had to pry my fingers from the edge of my chair. I had never felt terror like that in my life. Well, many years later I had the good fortune to study with Tito Gobbi in a master class; I'm a baritone now. He and Senora Gobbi had a little welcome party at their home for a small group of us selected to study with him. I had a couple of glasses of wine and got my courage up, and I said, 'Maestro Gobbi, I've always wanted to tell you about the first opera I went to and what an incredible experience it was; you were in it and it changed my life, but you scared the hell out of me that night.' And he looked very intently at me, and suddenly this very fat, jovial man looked straight into my eyes; this incredible look of malevolence came over him for five or six seconds. He struck absolute terror into this twenty-five-year-old boy. He had done what he wanted to do; he slapped me on the back and said, 'See, kiddo, it's only acting!' "

THIS IS THE WORLD I SEE

What satisfies me most is the creativity I discover in the callers. Regardless of age or situation, I hear them trying to make something useful out of their own experiences. Like composers, they weave words and gain gradual insight from playing with a phrase; like sculptors, they pare away until an essence is revealed; like painters, they work and rework something until they settle on the right image, saying, in effect, this is the world that I see. And they do it all live, in front of thousands of other people. What I do is give them a roomy hothouse to thrive in, a welcoming and safe place to unfold.

Sometimes I am so intrigued with a listener's story that I want to say, "Tell me everything about your life," but there isn't time, the caller vanishes into air, just as he or she appeared out of the air. I knew instantly from Kathleen's lovely voice that she must be a performer. In describing one of her own cherished experiences, she told me about her performance at one of the most important theatrical venues in America, the Kennedy Center in Washington, D.C., where she was appearing before four thousand people in a production of the opera *L'incoronazione di Poppea*. The show had a very special look to it, including a forty-five-degree rake to the stage that wound up near the first row of seats. It was here that the director asked Kathleen, playing Ottavia, to stand and sing two horrendously difficult but marvelous arias. "The director told me to make the aria more personal by thinking of saying good-bye to someone I deeply cared about. During the performance, I hadn't sung more than four or five measures when the woman seated right in front of me started to cry. The more I got into the aria the more I could feel her anguish and pain, and then the most amazing thing happened. As the tears were running down her face, she started to move forward in her seat until she was an arm's length away from me. I reached out and— remember, I'm still trying to get out all the high notes— she touched my hand. The rest of the aria was sung with the two of us holding hands. Everyone in the theater just gasped over the fact that this could happen, that a singer would take the hand of an audience member in the Kennedy Center. She was out of her seat and gone by the time of the curtain call, and I never saw her again."

CHAPTER TWO

Still a Loving World

I listen *for* things in people as much as I listen *to* them. And after many years of doing so, what I have come to understand is that goodness is contagious. The more I ask for stories about their attempts to live meaningful lives, the more courageous and authentic the callers seem to become. Whether they are new or regular listeners, they try to say what they mean and to speak from the best part of themselves.

The diversity of our callers is expected but extraordinary. When the phone rings on the air, I hear from people working in just about every profession, from mentally disabled citizens living in the community, straight and gay people, war veterans, people of color, famous people, unemployed citizens, those who live with AIDS, people on welfare, and those who have more money than they will ever need. We receive our share of grouchy, mean-spirited callers, too, and they get a fair hearing like everybody else.

I'm not interested in embarrassing people, whether

we agree or disagree. It is possible to have tremendous intimacy on the air without exploiting people to get it. I admire the courage it can take when a first-time caller dials a number to who knows where and says, "I'm nervous, I've never done this before." I ask them to imagine sitting around a kitchen table with me.

I believe our listeners often participate, as I do, as an act of service to one another and maybe even to something greater than themselves.

The simple truth is that, in the end, no one can force listeners to call, to give of themselves as much as they do. They alone make that choice and deserve credit for doing it.

One afternoon, in the middle of a stream of adult callers who were discussing how to turn a deficit in your life into an asset, I said, "You're on the air," and heard a young voice announce that his name was Ethan. Our conversation went like this.

❦

ETHAN: I'm eight years old. I got scapegoated and now I'm in another school and it really helps me with my self-confidence and self-control. Bye!

FAITH: Ethan, wait. Can I ask you a question? You said you were scapegoated, why?

ETHAN: Because I was different, because I have learning disabilities and they thought they were smarter than me, that's why.

FAITH: And what did you figure out?

ETHAN: I figured out that I'm better than them at some things, and they're better than me in others.

FAITH: What are the good strong things that you have?

ETHAN: Science and my writing ability.

FAITH: How about talking?

ETHAN: I talk too fast.

FAITH: But you're a good talker, right?

ETHAN: Yeah, but I talk too fast.

FAITH: Well, okay, but you have good thoughts.

ETHAN: Yeah, but I have trouble getting it down on paper.

FAITH: We're talking about what your strengths are. So, even though the kids at the first school were bad to you, you had to sit down with yourself and think, well, what's good about me, right?

ETHAN: Yeah.

FAITH: And you have a good sense of that now, that's great. Do you have some friends, Ethan?

ETHAN: Yeah, in my new school practically every kid is my friend. I have tons of friends on the bus, too.

FAITH: I'm glad you called. I can hear all the special things in you; bye, Ethan.

ETHAN: Bye.

QUITE A LADY

Although I am continually amazed at the way listeners have paid tribute in public to someone important in their lives, one story stands out, because the woman who phoned us has been battling her own mental illness for many years. I recognized in her voice a certain calm that I hear in those who have found a way to adjust to difficulty. I guessed Ann was in her seventies.

"I hope I can explain myself clearly. I was married in the 1960s and had three children. During this period I was hospitalized three times for mental illness, yet my husband always said to the children, 'Your mother is ill, she had to go away.' His family always took in my children while I was away, sometimes for as long as a year."

I could still hear sadness, and real compassion, when Ann described the end of this marriage.

"After twelve years, I more or less divorced this man, and it was a slap in the face to his family. A year later my condition was such that I had to assign him custody of my children. He raised them with a new wife for the next fifteen years, and during that time he faithfully brought the children to me on the holidays. He never said a word against me; he never said, 'Your mother is crazy.' He didn't understand it and yet he didn't degrade what he didn't understand. None of us really understood; I don't myself to this very day. I thought that was a pretty gentlemanly thing for him to do."

TWINS

I read more newspapers than the average person does because I can't resist and because I'm searching for moments in ordinary lives that grab my attention. Often I find them in the middle of a story, or in a tiny story at the bottom of a page.

In an old *Boston Globe* I noticed a small obituary about identical twins who had lived together most of their lives; one of them had just died. Several months later, still curious, I began searching for the surviving twin, enlisting the help of several telephone operators. I finally made contact and, to this day, I recall the story he told on the air in an Irish accent.

"I'm an identical twin and my brother and I lived together every day we were alive, except for six months when he was in the military." I tried to reconcile the sweetness of his manner with the enormity of his loss. These identical twins had spent almost every minute of their lives together for more than seventy years. I learned that they were devoted to the Boy Scouts, and that they could always find something to laugh about over the years. I was unprepared for what I heard next. When I asked him how he was managing to cope with his loss, he said, "The hardest part is shaving. I look in the mirror and I see my brother."

HE WAS ME

I heard one more story about twins three months later. Carrying a mug of hot chocolate with me into the studio, I sat down, frustrated; I had just spent the afternoon puzzling over how to handle a woman, obviously a drunk, who would repeatedly call our office's answering machine in the middle of the night, leaving confused, nasty messages that were usually fifteen minutes in length.

The first caller to the show was a man named Joe, who sounded like he was around thirty. "I'm adopted, an only child. I've never been one to pursue my roots because I've been very content with the upbringing I've had. But a few years ago I was in a lounge with my wife. I looked over and there was a person that was me."

At first I wasn't clear about what Joe meant. "He was my twin," he said, "somebody who resembled me so much it was like looking in a mirror. You always hear that somewhere on the planet there is supposed to be an identical person for each of us; mine was ten feet away from me. The experience was unnerving because I started thinking about being adopted. Could this be a twin brother I didn't know about? So I sat there and we exchanged glances. I said to my wife, 'Should I go up to him and say hello? Should I ask, do you see what I see? Is it as strange to you as it is to me?' "

I asked Joe if the man seemed to recognize him or show any signs of having the same reaction. "Yes, through a glance that said, this is kind of strange. But neither of us made an effort to approach the other. When I finally built up my courage to introduce myself, I turned and he was gone. To this day I can't help driving by the spot, wondering, is this person here somewhere? Was this my imagination? I know it wasn't because my wife confirmed it."

WALL OF MEMORY

Ken was in his early seventies and his voice was still filled with enthusiasm for what he does. He told me he constructed a section of his tiny hamburger joint from buildings destroyed in the 1960s as part of the city's so-called urban renewal plan. "They were tearing down places the workers and residents had given their lives to. Where were they gonna go? So what I did was, I went and took one brick from every one of those businesses and homes they demolished and I used them to create this wall." And then Ken described his greatest pleasure. "I watch the people from the old neighborhood come in, sometimes with a grandchild in hand, and they point at the wall, saying, 'There's my brick.' Lots of times I see a tear coming down the guy's face."

HANG ON

A younger voice greeted me on another afternoon, identifying herself shyly as Mary Lou. She sounded completely genuine. Like Ken's, her story had its roots in the sixties, when she was just a girl showing up at a basement dance party. "The local boys had formed a new band and they played a classic song of that era, 'Hang On Sloopy,' over and over again. I noticed the lead singer in the band, an adorable blond hunk of a nineteen year old, who winked at me and came up to me afterward. There I was, just fourteen, and just getting interested in boys. The singer had dropped out of college and was staying with a cousin in the area. We saw each other whenever they were playing at a party somewhere."

She hesitated, then said, "I just never got over him. About a year later, he was drafted and went to Vietnam and was killed. I still have the newspaper clipping with his photo in an old wallet somewhere in the attic."

The last thing Mary Lou told me I remember sometimes when I am trying to describe the nobility I hear in many of the callers to my show. "Not long ago, I went to the Vietnam Memorial in Washington; I brought a copy of 'Hang On Sloopy' and left it at the wall with a note near his name."

CHAPTER THREE

Life Line

No single device has helped us more in conveying how we feel, who we are, or who we wish we could be than the telephone, my favorite invention. It has carried all the big and little stories of our lives to friends and strangers around the world. Even as I sometimes wish it would shut up and go away, I don't mean it; I would be miserable without it.

My love of the telephone is symbolized by my sister's sixteenth birthday gift to me, a sterling charm bracelet with a single charm—a telephone, commemorating an incident during my junior year at George J. Penney High School. It was the rage then to select a member of the opposite sex to be your "brother," a kind of associate best friend. I picked Paul Seely, a great guy. On the afternoon in question, Paul and I began a single telephone conversation that lasted seven straight hours. I was grounded for a hundred years, but deep inside I swaggered over my new phone chops. Obviously, it was only the beginning.

I once had a call-in show about the telephone itself,

and it produced one of the most interesting times I've experienced on the air.

We were discussing the history of the phone, including how the first phone company tried to get the public to use the phone greeting "ahoy, ahoy" instead of "hello." We heard what it was like in the days of party lines and you had to share one line with as many as fifteen other families. (You listened to the number of rings to tell if it was for you.) And we brought up the subject of working conditions for phone operators in the early days; they sat on stools so close together that if one operator got a cold, so did all the rest. In fact, it was this conversation about operators that sparked the interest of a listener named Susan.

She began her story by announcing that she was standing outside while she talked to me; I didn't realize the importance of her location until later. As her tale unfolded, Susan talked faster and faster, mimicking the situation she described. "I am an operator with Southern New England Telephone now but I wanted to tell you a story about when I worked as an operator in Utah. They asked you to be real quick with every caller, just a few seconds at most, or else. I'm working away and I get this frantic call from a lady. A big prairie fire was raging and it had gone past her house and then doubled back. All the fire engines were way out in the desert fighting the fire, and she was there baby-sitting six children. She said her front and back porches were on fire, and so were the bushes all around the house. I could hear the kids in the background screaming. She was frantic, and I kept her on the line while I tried all the fire departments. Couldn't get through to anybody. Tried any place I could think of but I couldn't get anyone to come and help. I was racking my brain and all of a sudden I thought, what about the regular news service that sends the traffic helicopters out. I called a newspaper that uses one and they got the pilot who happened to be in the building. He ran upstairs, jumped in the helicopter, flew out and . . ."

Susan's telephone line went completely dead at this point. In the studio, we looked at one another in disbelief. And then the listeners and I heard that familiar computerized voice: "Deposit sixty-five cents, PLEASE." She was at a pay phone.

It was a fabulous moment, one I couldn't have dreamed up. I waited, trying desperately not to laugh in the middle of such a dramatic story, and I heard, plunk, plunk, plunk, plunk. Talk about grace under pressure: Susan delivered a single-word apology, "Sorry," and went racing on with her story right where she left off. "So she's screaming, saying smoke is coming through the windows and under the door, and I'm giving her instructions, to go wet towels in the back of her toilet tank and put them under the door, but don't get water on the window glass because it will explode and crack. She's yelling these commands to the kids to do all this as they're screaming, and over her line I can hear the pilot radioing where she is to the fire trucks. Soon over her phone line I could hear the fire engines in the distance and then there's all this commotion and she's screaming, 'They're here, they're here! We're saved!' And then I hear click. Just like that she disappeared."

I thanked this operator for what she did. And I can tell you she is hardly alone in her instinct to respond generously.

One day I simply invited listeners to tell me about "the other side of the news," the big and small accomplishments in their lives. Calls poured in, and more than anything else, I was struck by the eagerness I heard in so many voices. Rudy, a sixty-seven-year-old retiree, sounded like he could barely believe his good fortune. "Not long ago, when I retired, I knew five languages and I was at a loss about what to do." He and his wife enrolled in a course to learn Yiddish. They made many Jewish friends, and when they discovered that Russian Jews were immigrating to the area, they volunteered three days a week to teach them English. "These Russians were the intelligentsia, yet they knew almost nothing about their own religion because they weren't allowed to practice their faith in Russia. There I am, a gentile, and I'm doing all this research to teach them how Passover originated and is celebrated. My life is so full all the time."

STRIPPERS IN ANOTHER ROOM

*D*arby said that her hands were sweating as she placed the call to me because she had never phoned a radio show before. She began tentatively but as she spoke her voice became more and more confident. "I'm a construction worker, and there was going to be this Christmas party in about three months. The guys started asking me if I would go, even though they planned to have strippers there. I said no, because I didn't want to be around that. I thought that was the end of it, but the guy organizing the party kept saying he wanted it to be for the whole crew and he offered that the strippers could be in another room or that I could leave early. I told him that I'd just be pretending. Finally, he put it to a vote and the crew voted not to have the strippers. I had a great time. I stayed the whole night and the organizer hugged me at the end."

FEAR OF WORDS

A young caller, Eric, who was perhaps in his early twenties, was a good example of the courage it takes to overcome fear. First, he described himself as an under-achiever in school, who almost didn't graduate, but he soon realized that his real problem was that he couldn't stand reading. "I used to get panic attacks in libraries, and I had a real mental block about looking up words in the dictionary." Two years ago, Eric said, he decided to slow down and try looking up words. "I've actually begun to enjoy it and realize the beauty, you might say, of words and their definitions." Eric now produces an instructional drawing show on cable TV, revolving around words and their definitions, which he draws. When I asked him for an example, he said, "With the word *malevolent,* let's say, I draw people being angry or wishing ill will to others, which I think is how Webster defines it. I never thought I could overcome any of this. People would always ask me if I'd read a certain book and I'd say, nah, I don't read much. But I've been able to turn this around. My high school English teacher just asked me to come talk to the class. It's amazing the person I've become, and, actually, I like it. My show plays Friday nights on cable in New York City."

LIFE IN ONCOLOGY

A professional pianist named Hank got through and explained how he decided to cure his own sense of isolation by registering for a community program that coordinates artist visits at local hospitals. "Every Friday afternoon I take the elevator to the fifth-floor oncology unit of Yale New Haven Hospital. I play the piano they have in the solarium and patients from all over the world come and sit down. It's remarkable to make a connection with them." Hank had just moved to the area and hoped his experience would allow him to get to know people. As he signed off, he said, "I've made so many friends I can hardly believe it."

CHAPTER FOUR

Appreciating Older Sisters

When I hear politicians talk about cutting social security payments to children of deceased parents, I am dismayed by the cruelty of the notion. My own parents died when I was in high school, and there was no insurance money. Without those modest social security benefits and low-interest government loans, I couldn't have gone to college.

I was admitted on scholarship to a small, excellent state school, Eastern Connecticut State University, and I will always be grateful to them because they ignored my mediocre grades and took a chance on me.

The first year was crucial. While handling the loss of my parents, I was adjusting to a new home and trying to make new friends. At times I wondered where I belonged, and then I would think of my sister Sally, thirteen years older than me. In these years especially, she became my best friend.

She encouraged me to call her every week, and to come to her little house on weekends, where she and her family turned the closet-size sewing area into "Faith's Room." During our long, frequent telephone calls she would listen carefully to all my stories and take such pleasure in every accomplishment I revealed in the hope of making her proud. She was the person in my life whose devoted attention at such an important time steadied and energized me.

One Christmas, I invited Sally to join me on the air to ask listeners for stories about older sisters. Was it chance that brought such great callers to the show? More likely it was that we explained the "mothering" that older sisters sometimes do. Something important happened on the air that day, and I think my sister and I will remember it always.

A caller named Caroline told us a story about her older sister, Pauline. "Pauline was eight years older than I was, and she was very protective of me; she was as much my mother as my sister." When Caroline had been just five years old, she could barely contain her excitement as her big sister helped her into the thick leggings that children wore in those days to keep warm, and the pair set off for a grown-up afternoon of shopping and lunch downtown.

As darkness fell, Pauline realized it was time to catch the return bus home. The doors opened; Pauline helped Caroline up the steps of the packed bus, and they were forced to ride standing in the well. As the bus wound its way through the downtown streets, the lamp lights and sparkling store windows cast a magical glow. Their street was the first stop, and as the rubber-edged doors whooshed open, Pauline stepped off first to help her sister down. "The bus was so crowded," Caroline remembered, "and I was so short that the driver couldn't see me. My sister had my hand, and she was outside the bus when the doors closed on my arm."

At that moment, all of us in the studio stopped moving and listened intently. As the old bus crawled slowly away from the curb, Pauline ran beside it, refusing to let go of her little sister's hand. "I know that she would have held on to my hand no matter what." The bus stopped when a passenger saw what was happening and shouted to the driver, and the girls were unhurt.

Our phones rang steadily that afternoon. Tom's voice was bright, without a trace of sadness. What I think I heard in that voice was someone who understands the value of what he has. "My sister raised and mothered my brother and myself, and she wasn't that much older than us, four or five years at most. It was hard to listen to her all the time because sometimes I would think, she's only my sister. See, we didn't have an easy childhood. My dad shot my mother in the head when we were young. It was a horrible thing to live through. Our sister had to take over and she helped us put those memories away. She would, like, make Christmas wonderful for us, and make sure that we stayed on the right track. When my father went to prison, all three of us went to live with an aunt. My sister stuck up for us like you wouldn't believe. One time there was this neighborhood fight; my brother and I were getting picked on by three other guys, and my sister ran out of the house with a Wiffle ball bat and swatted them all away. I still talk to her every day. It's just touching to know someone like her."

Like Tom, a caller named Paul knew he gained something valuable, despite recent hardship in his life. He wasn't bragging when he told his story, he was appreciative. "I had a successful business I built for twenty-five years and I lost it last year. I also have four incredible sisters; one of them let me live with her, and another sister helped me out financially. Just as I was dialing your number, the sister I live with came downstairs with coupons for food for my dog. My sister and her husband fixed up this basement for me and it's beautiful. I was living before in my own fifteen-room house. I'm much happier here in the basement. When anyone comes to visit upstairs, naturally they tromp downstairs so I get lots of company. I am so fortunate."

🌿

When the next caller, Tina, reached us, I was amazed to hear her say in a soft, composed voice that she had just woken up in a psychiatric hospital. "I'm suffering from severe depression that started twenty months ago when I remembered being raped by a neighbor. I had ECT [electroconvulsive therapy] today for the first time, which made me sleep, and I awoke to the sound of your voice talking about the gift of a sister. It makes me remember Martha."

Just using her sister's name made Tina's voice more animated. "She's three years older than I am but she was never a big sister who pushed me away. When we were little, she was always a source of joy and support. If I was having trouble sleeping, she'd make up poop recipes so I could laugh and fall asleep. And now, when my life is literally depending on my staying well, she sends me flowers and calls me all the time. And at times when I've gotten shaky, she's flown up here at the drop of a hat. As black as it has gotten, it has taken my breath away to realize how supportive my whole magnificent family has been. And thank you for letting me publicly acknowledge what a heartmate my sister is to me. I'm a blessed woman and I am going to get well."

CHAPTER FIVE

Words to Live (and Die) By

After reading that author E. M. Forster wanted his ashes scattered wherever he happened to be at the time of his death, I began imagining the possibilities. The supermarket checkout line, the dentist's chair, a Hertz rental car.

When "Shep" Nuland's fascinating book *How We Die* won the National Book Award, a nationwide conversation about how much we can be in control of death began. And to honor those who would like to be controlling right up to the very last minute, my friend Bob Gregson and I invited listeners to design their own tombstone epitaphs. The phone lights began flashing immediately.

The first woman to reach us wanted her tombstone to say, "Therapy Didn't Help." We punched up the second line and heard from a man who has had his fill of New Age promises. He wants his stone to read, "A Perfect Example of Homeopathy at Work." Then a writer phoned to tell us he's known what his epitaph will be ever since he graduated from college as a literary writing major. "My name will be on the stone followed by the word 'Writer,' and beneath that it will say, 'A Decent Plot at Last.'"

Bob and I began discussing what a shame it is that you have to miss your own funeral. On line four an entomologist told us his tombstone would say, "Still Collecting Bugs."

A man from Wakefield, Rhode Island, had no interest in his own epitaph, but he wanted to lend one to any dentist who might be listening: "Here Lies So and So, Filling His Last Cavity."

To finish the hour, Bob promised his own tombstone would read, "Elvis Says Hi."

PASS IT ON

Many of us know, when we examine our own lives, that despite our reasonable fears, "the kindness of strangers" is constant.

A simple example: When I was in a little coffee shop in Provincetown, on Cape Cod, Massachusetts, a woman ordered a large coffee and a cranberry muffin to go, then realized that her wallet was empty. I overheard her and paid her bill with a few singles I had stuffed in my pocket; it was no big deal. When she asked for my address, I just said, "Pass it on."

The next evening, my sister, Sally, joined me on vacation, and when she pulled into the metered parking lot, she realized she had no quarters. She stood by the meter for a minute, trying to figure out her next move, and an older woman came out of the cottage adjacent to the lot and said, "I bet you need quarters." When my sister nodded yes, the woman said, "Here you go," and dumped eighteen quarters into my sister's hands. Sally tried to pay her, but the woman waved her off, saying as she walked away, "That's okay, do it for somebody else." After hearing the story, I laughed; it always comes back to you, I just didn't know it would happen so fast.

A good friend suggested that I ask listeners for wise sayings, like "Pass it on." But, later, when I told an acquaintance that I planned to do the show, she smirked about "how eager the public is to live inside a sappy greeting card." I see it, of course, another way. We are hungry for ideas to live by, and the eagerness for this sort of guidance is, in fact, a smart response to a world that frowns on stories which are positive or encouraging. Our listeners were quick to express their gratitude for words of advice from teachers, relatives, neighbors, friends, and in Thomas's case, someone he never met. "In 1947, I was a student at Brooklyn Technical High, a building covering six square blocks that housed about a thousand of us. Three of us were walking down the stairs and we had the disease I call senioritis; we thought we were kings of the world. On the fourth-floor level we became aware of a teacher on the stairs behind us, one of the few black teachers in the school. We were walking three abreast and even though we were conscious he wanted to get by, we were seniors, nobody gets by. Finally, I heard his sonorous voice say from behind us, 'Boys, you know it's not always those who oppose you that stop you, but those who are going in the same direction more slowly.' At eighteen, I didn't recognize the importance of what he said. It has come back to me many times over the years."

❦

A man named Marcus told about how frustration turned out to be useful for him. "In the late seventies I began working with geriatric patients who had severe problems, Like Alzheimer's and strokes. I found I wasn't very effective." Marcus learned the hard way that the things you find in textbooks don't always fit in life. "I met a remarkable woman in the course of this venture. Aside from the personal life she was living at the time— she had two severely impaired parents, two children with chronic diseases, she had unemployed family members, she was running the whole household—she found time to be encouraging to just about everyone she met. When I found out that things weren't working out as I'd planned, she would say to me from time to time that 'despair is a luxury we cannot afford.' That has come back to me as a great source of strength over the years."

Marcus reminded me of someone I deeply respect,

newswoman Charlayne Hunter-Gault, who helped pave the way for other African Americans to be able to attend white colleges in the South. When I asked her what it cost her to endure the racial epithets thrown at her at such a young age, she said, "I learned from Dr. Martin Luther King Jr. that the struggle is ennobling."

We also heard from a caller named Mercy, who introduced herself as a symphony orchestra conductor and concert pianist. She said, "For women, it's not particularly easy to make headway in a career like mine. I had a wonderful teacher, Charles Brook [Bruch?]. Once we were discussing the possibilities of my career and Maestro Brook said to me, 'Well, how do you think that you're going to be able to make it in the world?' And I said, 'A lot of hard work and a lot of study.' And he said to me, 'Tell me something, Mercy, who wins the war?' And I thought it was a little bit off the beaten track, what he was asking me, but I said to him, 'Well, Maestro, the strongest one.' But he said, 'No, guess again.' 'Okay,' I said, 'the sneakiest one, the wisest one.' He said, 'No, that's not true either.' Then I said to him, 'The one who is in the right.' And he said, 'No, wrong again. It is the one who lasts the longest. If you can hold your breath, and not forget your goals, and you can hang in there, you will be successful. But don't expect success to come to you easily because there are many obstacles.' "

Like the caller, I was consoled with a saying repeated by one of my dearest friends, Bruce Clements. When he learned that I was worrying about money, he explained that when he was a boy he asked his mother, a struggling single parent, if they were rich. She answered, "Yes, we're rich; we have everything we need."

I put this answer on a slip of paper on my refrigerator —my own "Hallmark card."

CHAPTER SIX

Bats, Hiccups, and Wings

I was moderating an animal rights debate in a crowded auditorium at Yale University, when I heard myself say, "Let's go with that suggestion and kill two birds with one stone." Everyone in the room looked stricken.

These words probably flew out of my mouth in reaction to the person who had just risen from his chair to propose that we stop buying honey "because it exploits worker bees."

At least we weren't being broadcast live. Every broadcast interviewer I know tries to prepare for the variety of unexpected things that happen during a live show, but the truth is that no amount of preparation can prevent some things from occurring. Like the day during one of our on-air fund-raising drives that I sat in my chair, opened the mike, and began talking with one eye fixed on a bat, which was in the process of squeezing through the ceiling heat vent. While dodging the swooping bat, I continued to explain how delighted I would be to send every donor one of our embossed coffee mugs. The bat attached itself to the wall just six inches from the back of my head. I spent the next six and a half minutes singing the praises of public radio while the voice in my head said, "I know it's going to nest in my HAIR."

The bat episode, of course, did not mark the end of my experience with the unexpected during live shows. In fact, one winter afternoon, just thirty minutes before airtime, I developed hiccups. I wasn't upset until fifteen minutes later when I realized they were still with me. I raced out to the producer and managed to explain in jerky sentences that I could be in trouble.

His surefire solution was to have me close my eyes and stand next to the massive steel studio door, which he slammed shut with all his strength, hoping to scare me out of my predicament. I was scared all right. We waited silently on opposite sides of the door, and then the hiccups started again. And when I tried to open the steel door to report that it hadn't worked, the handle wouldn't turn. The slamming door trick had jammed the lock and now I was trapped in the wrong studio with just fifteen minutes left before air. First I screamed through the door that I couldn't get out, and then I had to plan exactly how to break this fascinating bit of news to the station manager.

Luckily, Charm's Locksmith took pity on the producer's hysterical phone plea. They quickly dispatched a locksmith who had the door off its hinges with three minutes to spare, no charge. I was doing a live interview with the ambassador to somewhere but I don't recall a word that was said, only that several minutes into the interview it dawned on me that my hiccups had disappeared.

Obviously, these were events that I didn't cause and so they have a charming serendipity to them. But there was one awkward moment that I can't blame on chance or anyone else.

I very much wanted to finish up a story I'd been working on about the difference between old-fashioned Chinese restaurants and the more modern Chinese restaurants run by the sons and daughters of the original owners, who had introduced America to Chinese cuisine. The interviews with the children, who spoke and understood English perfectly, went smoothly. Unfortunately, I could not find an English-speaking owner to represent the older generation. But after I'd returned from a big birthday lunch for one of my colleagues, I found a message on my desk indicating that the owner of a traditional Chinese restaurant would see me. I grabbed my tape recorder and jumped in the car.

I pulled up in front of an old-fashioned restaurant and at two o'clock I was the only person in the place. The owner, who spoke English tentatively, gestured for me to sit down in one of his red vinyl booths, which I did cheerfully. He then whipped out a large red menu and said, "You eat now," and disappeared while I tried to make a selection. Just this one interview to go, I said to myself; the man wants me to eat, I'll eat as a sign of respect. Except that I was so stuffed from the noontime birthday party that every dish seemed extreme. I searched for the smallest thing I could find. "Wings, please," I said.

"Wings," he said, bowing slightly before dashing off to the kitchen to prepare my meal. He reappeared in no time with a huge platter of chicken wings and, proudly setting it down before me, he bowed slightly and returned to the kitchen.

I dutifully picked up the first wing and began eating. It was no use. I was nauseated by the idea of eating another bite. How not to offend my host and ruin my interview? I instantly dumped the platter of wings into my napkin, folded it fast, and whipped it into my handbag. I sat there a little stunned. Ten minutes or so later my host reappeared.

"Delicious!" I said, triumphantly, glancing up into his face. And with that each of us looked down at the empty platter. There were no chicken bones.

"Yes," he said, smiling oddly.

"Yes," I said, "REALLY delicious." He graciously whisked away the empty platter without a word.

At the register, after paying my bill, he answered all my questions and I hurried to the car to see about the mess in my bag.

🌿

As the chicken wing story points out, an interest in goodness has little to do with living anything resembling a perfect life. I love our radio community as much for its eclectic cast of expressive and sometimes mischievous characters. There was the James Dean fan who had a dummy of the star made and drove it around in the passenger seat of his convertible. I remember the woman who called to say she had a terrible fear, and when we all leaned forward to hear it, she added, "of salad bars." And there was the shipyard welder, a sweetheart of a guy, who turned his suburban backyard into a fabulous life-size dinosaur theme park, open free of charge to anyone who happens by.

When I considered doing a show in which we would ask listeners to tell us about something they got away with, I started considering my own mischief list. For starters, it includes speeding, lying, exaggerating, hypocrisy, and pretending.

Let me be more specific about an incident that was unplanned. Every year near Thanksgiving, the chef at Eastern Connecticut State University would somehow convince a few students to dress up like Pilgrims and Indians and stand around picturesquely while all the other students lined up for helpings of the large roasted turkeys and hams that were beautifully displayed.

One year, my friends and I were conscripted for cleanup duty. As the evening drew to a close, each of us was handed a huge heavy platter containing an untouched baked ham or turkey; we were asked to march in a straight line with them down the hall and into the kitchen. I marched as I was told except that when the line veered right I spontaneously veered left and my friends and I wordlessly paraded off with the twenty-pound cooked ham.

I don't know why I wanted a big ham and I wasn't exactly sure what to do with it once we had it upstairs in our dorm room. Someone suggested locking it in one of our suitcases, which seemed completely reasonable at the time. Then, like all crooks, we made a plan. The plan was to race off to the store, buy bread, mustard, and beer, and prepare for the next night's magnificent feast. We were unprepared for what greeted us the next morning as we passed through the breakfast line with as much innocence as we could display. There next to the cash register was a big hand-lettered sign that said, simply, WE KNOW WHO HAS THE HAM.

The cashier eyed everyone suspiciously, or so we thought, convinced as only guilty people are that she was merely waiting to trap us. We fled to our room. There were individual meetings. We opened the suitcase and ripped off a few hunks of ham and shrieked at one another about what to do. There were larger group meetings, more noshing. We actually became scared because we were harboring a ham. What if they really KNEW? We looked at the ham, which now had some good-sized holes in it, and concluded that we would have to give it back. Rabbit, who looked the most like a graduate of Catholic school, was selected to sneak back in the middle of the night with the ham-filled suitcase, which she did. In line at breakfast the next morning the sign was gone; not another word was said. I still crave baked ham.

HIS BEAUTIFUL THINGS

I warned the producers that I wasn't sure listeners would call in to talk about what they had gotten away with, but I was wrong. After telling my Thanksgiving story, I went first to the woman who came up with the topic, Regina Barreca, author of *Sweet Revenge, the Wicked Delights of Getting Even,* and one of the most wonderful guests a talk show host could have. So, live on the air, I phoned her, demanding to know which of her own crimes she was prepared to reveal. Her story was also about Thanksgiving. "I had one fastidious, fancy uncle who we saw only once in a while, like on major holidays. He lived alone and he didn't like children or company. He was a Dickensian sort of character, locked away in his beautiful home with his beautiful things. Remember when holidays would take three or four weeks to get through? The grown-ups were talking and you couldn't understand how people could just sit around and talk. I went into my uncle's library and began looking through some beautiful nineteenth-century illustrated Audubon books. I tore out all of the pictures I liked. I folded them up into little pieces and put them into my sock. I absolutely wrecked those books without realizing it. I didn't mean to do it; they were just pretty pictures, I was bored, and it seemed to me that I would probably look at them more than my uncle ever would. I remember carrying those things around with me as a kind of guilty icon, through my whole life. I'm sure they're in the base-

ment of my house. I'm too horrified as an adult to throw
them away."

I opened the phone lines to callers and held my
breath. The lines filled immediately.

GATHERING INTEREST

*I*t isn't often that I become speechless on the air, but
I was when John told his story. "This comes under the
heading of a deep, dark secret. About seven years ago, I
moved to Connecticut. I consolidated a little checking
account and the sum total in it was $1,412.00. When I
moved, I had the bank wire-transfer that money from
the out-of-state account into my new account here in
Connecticut. Perhaps six months went by before I actually opened any of the bank statements. Of course, you
can imagine what was there. What they had done was
transfer $14,120.00. When the first bank statement I
opened indicated this, I had a glass of wine in my hand
and I thought, well, this is the time to give up wine. For
seven years I have had $14,120.00 in that account and
have never had any intention of using it, because the idea
of spending the rest of my life in jail doesn't strike me as
a good prospect."

I asked John if the money was still sitting in his account. "It's sitting there and gathering interest. It's never
been touched. I've never brought it to the bank's attention because I wondered how long, just out of curiosity,
it would take for someone to discover this. It has been

going on like this for seven years. One of these days, when the mood strikes me, I'll go down to the bank and have some fun with them. I just thought you might find this a rather interesting secret."

The next caller delivered her lines in a deadpan voice. "A few years ago, I lost $14,120.00 from my checking account." (We roared.) She then went on to describe an incident in her youth. "I was the only girl in a family of four and my younger brother was a troublemaker. One day my mother had to run to answer the phone, and she said, 'Don't touch that iron.' Somehow, in the same room as the iron, there was a plastic bag. I was about six years old, and I thought it would be real interesting to find out what would happen to a plastic bag that had been exposed to an iron. Naturally it stuck and started smelling. And just about that time my little brother was walking into the room, and my mother came back and said, 'Who did this?' I said, 'He did!' And he's looking like, 'What? Mommy, I didn't.' I acted like I didn't know anything about it. And I said, 'Oh, Tommy, how could you do that?' I never tried to make it up to him as a child because he was a brat. But as an adult, I feel so guilty about it. I finally admitted to him that I had let him take the fall for it and he didn't remember it at all. He was so used to getting in trouble. My mother vaguely remembers it and claims that she sort of thought I might have done it."

HEROES CAN LIE

*W*hen I heard the timbre of Jude's voice, which still carries his Portuguese roots, I knew he had something important—and serious—to say. "I had to stop the car and talk to you so I'm calling from a phone booth; if there's a lot of background noise, I apologize. This is an incident that happened thirty-eight years ago. It didn't happen to me but I was a witness. We had just come from Portugal and we were only here a year. Where we had to walk home we had to go across this little footbridge which crossed over the Park River. Well, these two kids that were neighbors of ours were playing ball and the ball inadvertently bounced over the rail and went down into the river and landed on the ice. So these two kids started talking to this other kid that was about my age and they kept on saying, 'Why don't you go get the ball; the ice is fine, you'll be okay, just go get the ball.' And this poor kid went down to get the ball and fell through the ice and drowned. The police came to investigate and these two kids stood up and said, 'We tried to stop him but he just insisted on going down.' So I ran home and told my parents. I said, 'Ma, they didn't do what they said. They're the ones who made him go down and get the ball!' But because we were Portuguese my parents said God would punish them. They said, 'Don't get involved; they're not going to believe us anyway.' No one listened to me. The two boys had their pictures on the front page of the *Hartford Times,* which reported, 'These heroes tried to save the poor little boy who drowned.' In fact, they were the ones who killed this poor kid. For the past thirty-eight years I've been carrying this story with me."

SMOKED HIM OUT

On her car phone Rita announced that she was stuck in traffic, which strikes me now as cosmic retribution. "One time, my husband had a meeting in Boston, and because he was going to drive there, I decided to take the bus to Boston so that we could ride back together. I sort of don't watch the clock carefully, so he left me with a dire warning not to miss this bus since he'd have no way to reach me. Well, as I pulled into the terminal, the bus pulled out. My heart just sank. I was driving an older truck, and I figured the only way I could catch up with the bus was to race to its next scheduled stop and get there before the bus did. I drove ninety miles an hour all the way. My radiator was getting hotter and hotter and the needle was rising higher and higher and my hood was steaming. I thought, as long as the truck goes I'm going to go! So I kept going. I pulled in just as the bus pulled in. My engine was just about in flames but I ran and got on the bus. Of course, I couldn't tell my husband what I had done. On the drive back together, we stopped to pick up the truck, and I mentioned to him that I thought it might be a good idea if he drove the truck because I had been having a little bit of trouble with it. He got in the truck, started out, and it died in the middle of the freeway; we had to have it towed. To this day, he doesn't know that I'm the one who ruined the truck engine. He thinks he did!"

IT WAS WRONG

Michelle admitted she continues to feel guilty about what happened to her twenty-five years ago. "I was young and a clerk in a clothing store. I hated my boss, I was contemplating quitting. A young woman would come in a couple of times a week to visit this beautiful white dress that she loved. She told me a story about how much she wanted it. On the spur of the moment I helped her steal it. She was wearing, like, a bomber jacket, and she was full-figured. I told her to go in the ladies' room and wrap the dress around her waist, put on her jacket, and I would walk her out to the front of the store. And I did. Not only do I feel guilty for having done it, I feel guilty for having involved her. I quit the next day."

I imagined the other woman replaying this story in her mind just as Michelle does. She said, "I think for both of us it happened very fast, but both of us knew it was wrong. I appreciate the opportunity to tell the world."

QUIET DISCIPLINE

It was two months past Kenny's sixteenth birthday and he had just gotten his driver's license. "I had a date and used my dad's brand-new Pontiac Bonneville, which was a convertible with a super-big V-8 engine and four-speed on the floor. It was quite a machine and it was his pride. I was coming home about three in the morning; the road was glazed with ice. I took a curve at a pretty good speed about a half mile from my parents' home and I didn't make it. I hit a utility pole, wrecking his brand-new car. You can imagine the feeling. I said to myself, 'What am I gonna do? There's nothing to do.' I had to go home, wake up my dad, and tell him the bad news. He said to me, 'Go to bed and we'll deal with it in the morning.' Of course, everyone found out about it. But not another mention of that event ever took place for the rest of my life. And my dad wasn't wealthy. I got away with it in the sense that I wasn't punished in the conventional way. My dad was a pretty hard-nosed fellow and quite a disciplinarian. But I learned a forceful lesson that no punishment could have ever conveyed. I have a daughter myself now and hopefully I'll be able to have the same kind of loving impact on her that my dad had on me with that example."

CHAPTER SEVEN

Looking Back

When I was ten years old, my mother and I went to Glasgow, Scotland, for my one and only visit with my eighty-year-old maternal grandmother. She was stout, beautiful, and kind. In the mornings, she served us hearty breakfasts of eggs, blood sausage, toast, and tea to fortify us against the damp cold. In the evenings, we were warmed by putting a few shillings in the heater on the wall, and though we had supper only a few hours earlier, she would send me out around ten to the fish-and-chip wagon as soon as she heard its bell. To this day I remember it as one of the most delicious meals anywhere, piping hot fish and fries wrapped only in newspaper and served just that way.

Some evenings we would eat our chips with my mother's sisters and their children, all of whom I was meeting for the first time. While the grown-ups visited, my cousins and I would run upstairs to the rooftop to play and talk. I remember that it was on that roof that I told my new cousins how in America my father was a sheriff and had shot fourteen men, and that I was a famous singer. To prove it, I stood under the stars and sang every word of "Love Me Tender" with conviction.

I know now that it can require more bravery to sit down and resurrect a real past, unsure of what images and feelings will erupt. The inspiration to do so can come from publishers who ask for memoirs, or from children who want an elder's life story. For Brunhilda Cohan, a regular listener to our show, that inspiration apparently came from hearing a discussion I had on the air about farewells.

Now nearly seventy, Ms. Cohan is a master gardener and photographer. She can often be found crawling through her beautiful Connecticut gardens in search of the perfect rose. One afternoon, I opened a letter from Ms. Cohan, who said that after listening to our show she had been moved to write her first account of what happened to her at the age of sixteen in Hamburg, Germany, during World War II. I was immediately interested in the style of her handwriting, which seemed old-world. With her permission, I offer her remarkable story.

Dear Ms. Middleton,

I am thinking of a day which changed my life forever. The day was July 27, 1943, later known in Hamburg, Germany, as the day of the great catastrophe. I was sixteen at the time. Summer vacation from school had started and I was a little sad because my parents thought it best for me to stay home. . . . My parents, too, had given up their vacation plans because of the dangerous time we lived in. Hamburg had been bombed heavily already and my father explained that he needed me in case our apartment building received a phosphorous bomb. He thought that the two of us, with the help of asbestos gloves, could throw the bomb off the roof into the street below. I always knew he saw in me the son he never had.

On Sunday, the 25th of July, I was visiting my girlfriend Ursula, who lived a short distance from us. Her mother was busy washing and ironing and packing their suitcases. She told me that Ursula and she were leaving Hamburg the next weekend. They were to travel to Bavaria, the southern part of Germany, to a small town where they had reservations at a guesthouse. I still don't know how I had the courage to ask if I might travel with them. Ursula's mother said yes, if my parents gave me permission. Of course I would have to find my own accommodations when we got to Vilsbiburg, that was the name of the little town.

At dinner that night I brought up the subject of traveling to Bavaria with my girlfriend and her mother. All my father could say was that my place was with him right there in Hamburg, but my mother gave me a certain smile and a very faint nod as if to say we'll talk about it later. We did talk when I helped her with the washing up of the dishes. I told my mother that I didn't need much money, for I had saved up enough to cover the cost of the train ticket. She gave me a hug and assured me she also had some savings for me to use as I saw fit.

The next morning bright and early I rang the doorbell to my girlfriend's apartment, and after a little while, the buzzer sounded which enabled me to open the front door. I think I must have flown up the stairs, for I was so excited that I could travel to Bavaria. For obvious reasons I did not mention my father's refusal. Ursula's mother said, "We'll go tomorrow if you two can get the permits today." Anybody who wanted to leave Hamburg needed a permit to exit the city. Ursula and I ran to the elementary school [where we received the permits], and I dashed home to pack. Since it was summertime, I stuffed a few cotton dresses and shorts into my suitcase, and it took my mother quite some time to convince me to include a few heavy sweaters, just in case. And then my mother handed me an envelope to put into my handbag. It was the money she had saved and wanted me to have. When I started to look inside the envelope I noticed it contained a very large sum, more money than I had ever held in my hand. Somehow my mother knew I would eventually need it. But at age sixteen, I could only think of getting away from Hamburg, nothing was going to stop me.

On the morning of the 27th, Ursula and I had to take three heavy suitcases to the main Hamburg railroad station. I remember how we balanced them between our two bicycles and how every so often one of the suitcases would fall off because we didn't stay close enough together. It took us all morning to walk the four miles, but we made it and bought tickets for a train to leave that night at eleven o'clock. . . .

We had just hopped onto our bikes when the sirens began blasting. We followed people who were walking very fast and seemed to know where they were going. Sure enough, around the corner was an air-shelter. Above ground it looked like a brick round house, but once inside, one had to descend many steps to reach a large, rather dark and damp room. Such an air-shelter could hold hundreds of people. The stay in that smelly place was short, and when the sirens gave the all-clear sound everyone agreed that the enemy planes were headed for Berlin! Now we raced home and I was told to be at Ursula's front door at seven that night. Ursula's dad, who was one of the managers of the Hamburg Water Works, had a car and promised to drive us to the station. It was a company car and he was very reluctant to use it for private purposes, yet he felt he should make an exception. He was not allowed to leave the city because the water supply for a million people was of utmost importance.

I don't remember much about the afternoon, except that I tried to find my father, to ask for forgiveness, and to explain that I had to leave Hamburg. Also to tell him that I had never felt so strongly about anything before in my life. But my father was nowhere to be found, and when the time came for me to leave, I said good-bye to my mother, hugged and kissed her and thanked her. We were both crying and holding each other much longer than we would have if I were just going on a summer vacation. She handed me my new winter coat and then urged me to go. As I left the building, I looked up to the second floor, and there was my wonderful mother on our balcony bravely waving a large white handkerchief. I smiled and waved back, but when I reached the end of our street where I had to turn a corner, I waved once more and she was still waving to me. I stopped for a split second and thought, how can you leave your mother? And then I waved once more, turned the corner, and knew I would never see my mother again. The desire in me to live took over, and I walked as fast as I could to reach my friend's house. Ursula's father had started the motor and everyone was waiting for me. I climbed into the backseat, holding on to my bag and my new winter coat.

When we arrived at Hamburg Hauptbahnhof, the main train station, my girlfriend's father apologized that he could not wait with us and had to turn around right away. We said we understood and we all kissed him good-bye, even I. After a while more and more people joined us on the platform for the train to the south. At eleven p.m. sharp, just as our train was approaching, the sirens started to howl and when they stopped, a voice came over the loudspeakers: "Everybody into the underground shelters, please!" Nobody on our platform moved; the train had stopped, but when we tried to open the doors they were all locked. Suddenly, I saw a man lifting a little girl not much older than four or five, squeezing her through a very small window opening. He shouted to her to open the door, which she did. He climbed into the train and ran up and down opening doors. All this took fewer than three minutes; the platform was empty, and the train pulled out of the big hall. There were no whistles, no sign of a conductor, just utter silence and darkness. The train moved very slowly at first and only gradually picked up a little speed. I sat at a window with Ursula next to me. We held hands but didn't talk, as if a word from us would have given away our location. Ursula's mother sat opposite us and I think she prayed, silently. The train made its way through familiar suburbs and when we drove past the station where I had been many times on my visits to my grandparents, I looked out of the window, and lo and behold, what had been a dark night was now as bright as daylight. Hundreds and hundreds of green flowing objects that looked like Christmas trees were slowly falling out of the sky and were illuminating everything. We held our breath. And then we heard in the distance the dull sound of the impact of the falling bombs which made the earth shake and with it our train. Was a bomb going to fall on us, too? But the train kept rolling along, faster and faster.

After several hours of traveling through the countryside, Ursula and I embraced, we wept and we knew we had made it. Oh, how we kissed and hugged her mother, thanking her for saving us from a terrible fate. In Munich I sent, as promised, a card to my parents, telling them that I had arrived safely. What irony! It wasn't until a week later when Ursula's father came to Bavaria to spend a few days with us that we learned about the horrible catastrophe on the night of July 27th. Hamburg had been bombed so severely that a great firestorm had broken out which caused hurricane-like winds in the city of Bremen, seventy-five miles away. Ursula's father had escaped the tremendous heat and saved his life by standing up to his neck in a river under a small bridge across the street from where he had lived. He stood in the water for two and a half days, without sleep and without food. He didn't even dare drink the water, for he had used it. Seventy thousand people were killed in Hamburg in three days and nights of bombing. Nobody ever saw my parents again. After some years had passed, the government declared them dead.

I phoned Brunhilda Cohan's home after receiving her letter to say that I hoped writing it had been some comfort. On my desk I keep a picture of the rose she photographed and sent to me with her story.

CHAPTER EIGHT

Looking Ahead

Just as looking back can require courage, looking ahead can be a true test of faith. I appreciated the struggle for this faith in one of my guests, *Hartford Courant* columnist and WTIC radio talk show host Colin McEnroe, who joined me on the air for a show about adoption, a subject close to his heart.

Colin and his wife had just adopted their first child, a boy, Joey, and I asked Colin to read to our listeners the extraordinary letter he wrote to his new son on Father's Day.

> Dear Joey,
>   Once there was a guy. This guy and his wife couldn't have children. They tried for years and years. A lot of the time they were sad. Well, this guy and his wife began to talk about adopting children. But the guy wasn't sure. It took a long time for the guy to be sure, and even then he wasn't really sure. One day, a baby was born far

away. The guy and his wife got a phone call: "Your son is waiting for you." The guy got scared. The night before he was supposed to fly off and meet the baby, this guy drove around in his car in the rain, wondering if he was about to wreck his life and other lives, too.

The guy thought about the time of his life, how it was like a river, how he had been trying to steer a raft down it and now it seemed like the raft would just pinwheel off, unguided by him, toward a shore he couldn't see. But this guy had heard somewhere that when they hand you the baby, sometimes you just feel right away this fireball of love explode through you, and you know everything will be okay.

So he and his wife got on the plane and went to another city and found the hotel room and waited until the people there came with the baby. And they handed this guy a baby with dark shining eyes like no eyes the guy had ever seen. But what the guy felt most of all was fear, and there was no fireball, just a lot of confusion. The guy and his wife stayed in the hotel room for days, taking care of the baby. One day they went to another part of the city and met the woman who bore the baby and promised her they would love him.

But even saying those words this guy was worried, because there were a lot of diapers and bottles and blankets but no fireball. And everything the guy did with the baby felt like a mistake.

The guy and his wife and the baby flew home. Days and weeks went by and there was still no fireball, but now and then there were flashes and sparks and beams that lighted secret parts of the guy he didn't even know were dark.

Then the guy didn't feel like everything he did was a mistake. One day in the winter the guy's wife had to leave because her father died. The guy stayed home and took care of the baby for a week. All day long they played and he sang songs and cooked meals and talked about when Mama would come home. It was strange and sad because he was becoming a father, really a father, just when his wife lost hers. And he was growing close, really close to his son just when he was the loneliest he had ever been for his wife. Finally she came back and he was happy but that time lay inside of him like a wonderful, sorrowful dream. It changed him.

And today, do you know how this guy is today? Well, the fireballs of love swoop through him all the time. There's a fireball in the morning when his little boy wakes up, and one at night when his son goes to sleep. There are fireballs all day sometimes and the guy feels like the Fourth of July is happening inside him. And, sometimes,

when the guy is driving alone in his car, something rocks him, something stronger than a fireball. And the guy starts to cry because the feelings
inside were too big to turn into anything but tears.
Sometimes the guy will see another man with a
little boy and some bottles and blankets and diapers; this guy always smiles at the sight because he
thinks of his little boy at home. He thinks about
how great the bottles and blankets and diapers are,
how nice it is to use them. He wishes his little boy
were with him right now, wanting something to
drink. Or, he wishes he could go home right away
and listen to the birds in the yard with his wife
and his little boy.

Now it seems to the guy that the time of his
life is not like a river; it's like a great rustling tree
from which you can pluck all the fruits of delight.
So, Joey, if you are ever reading this many years
from now and wondering how this guy felt right
before Father's Day in 1991, you should know
that the guy felt okay. Yes, I think that would be
fair to say.

COMING FULL CIRCLE

*A*ppropriately enough, nine months after the adoption
show, a listener sent a letter that means so much to me.
On lined notebook paper, Nancy Rawn said,

Dear Faith,

Please excuse the stationery. I am writing to you from Cochabamba, Bolivia, and this is all I can find to write on at the moment.

I am sitting in a hotel room with my newly adopted Bolivian son and my husband napping nearby. I was gazing at the baby's beautiful face and jet black hair and recalling how this whole process of adoption started. I heard your show last spring, talking about how to begin an adoption, and was inspired to begin the process that my husband and I had been "talking about" for about four years.

The rest is history—through a lot of hard work and commitment on our part, and many other people's, we are here now with Jensen Phillipe, a beautiful ten-week-old Quechuan Indian boy. He truly needs a family and we truly want to make him a part of our lives.

So, I thought I'd come full circle and say thanks . . . your choice of speakers stirred our compassion and now our lives are so much richer for it. . . . Our radio community is bigger by one.

Gracias,

Nancy Rawn (and Jensen Phillipe)

CHAPTER NINE

Animal Nature

I think the listeners sense how much I delight in stories of trust and caring about animals, and they respond with terrific descriptions of their experiences in nature. A wonderful book, *The Biophilia Hypothesis* (Island Press, 1993), makes the case that the human urge to connect with the natural world, especially animals, is actually biological. My own philosophy differs from this—I like to think that we learn to respect and appreciate the natural world just as we learn compassion—nevertheless, the book is filled with scientists who are poetic in their essays about the passion they feel for other creatures. Edward Wilson writes, "The more we know of other forms of life, the more we enjoy and respect ourselves. . . . Humanity is exalted not because we are so far above other living creatures, but because knowing them well elevates the very concept of life."

I have been comforted throughout my life by special relationships with animals. At age eleven, my first pet was a parakeet named Budgie, who would fly down the hallway and perch on the inside knob of our apartment door at 3:30 each day to wait for me to come home from school. And when I did arrive, Budgie would flutter in the air until I held up my finger for him to land, and off we would go.

FIELDS OF HAPPY HORSES

On the day that I opened our lines to callers asking for their memorable experiences with animals, one of our frequent listeners phoned. Lifelong horse breeder Mary Jean Vasiloff reported to me that she continuously plays a radio tuned to our station in the big horse barn, and the minute my voice comes on welcoming listeners to the show, her Morgan horses whinny. Later, I visited these beautiful chestnut horses at the McCullogh Farm in Old Lyme, Connecticut, where Mary Jean taught me that if I stooped over, Groucho Marx style, so that I was on eye level with the colts, they wouldn't run away. Sure enough, when I did it, the colts would nuzzle me and let me stroke the soft skin on their chins.

I was in heaven walking through fields of green grass and graceful, happy horses, as Mary Jean told fascinating stories about her experiences breeding Morgans. My favorite was about a Morgan who was sick and having trouble trying to give birth. Mary Jean had been up so many cold nights with her that she decided to bed the horse down in her warm living room. The horse gave birth and convalesced there but the colt became so used to the living room that now and then during the ensuing year it would saunter in and flop down on the couch.

KATHARINE HEPBURN

*W*hen the North American Wildlife Rescue workers appeared on my show, Katharine Hepburn was apparently listening and later called the group to help her rescue a seagull with a broken wing. I'm told it was a chilly October morning when they arrived at Ms. Hepburn's waterfront home; the seagull was floating offshore. The rescuers were dismayed because they had not brought a boat. Who needs a boat, Ms. Hepburn replied. She just dove into the chilly waters of Long Island Sound, leaving the rescue people looking at each other onshore. The bird was treated and eventually released.

INTIMACY ON WINGS

*T*he first thing I noticed about Dennis when he called in was the wonder in his voice. I'd guess he was in his thirties, and I wish that what happened to him would happen to me.

Dennis moved from the city to the country and his house is across the street from a state forest. Taking up birding seemed like a natural thing to do. "One Sunday morning recently I got to some nice blueberry bushes and I sat down and waited. I saw a catbird and a few other semiexciting birds, when, suddenly, I heard a humming noise. To my joy, a hummingbird came buzzing out of the woods right up to me. I was wearing a bright red shirt; that's the only way I can explain it. It hovered two feet from my face for several minutes, just kind of looking at me. Then it landed on a branch next to me and sat there. I had never really seen a hummingbird up close. It was the most beautiful thing."

A USED DOG

A caller named Helena seemed to understand that animals can show us what counts in life. "My daughter was diagnosed as diabetic and everything seemed to be going wrong, and then we adopted a used dog from Golden Retriever Rescue. When we brought Walter home we thought, 'What are we doing? This is crazy.' But we have gained a very good friend. It sounds silly. He's only a dog, but he's a respected person and family member in our home." When I said to Helena that it sounded as if she was talking about believing in the unknown, she said, "That's it, it's possible to reach out and have faith in a dog you don't know."

BRAND CONSCIOUS

*R*oger phoned in to describe one of his shopping trips. "We drove a half hour from home into town in our Ford and the dog chased us, so we hid in the parking lot because we didn't want him to find us. He was sniffing tires only on Ford cars!"

BOOMER, WONDER DOG

One of the best times I've had reporting on animals was for my Connecticut Public Television series, *Sunday Drive*. I would take off in a vintage auto in search of great characters. One of them turned out to be a one-hundred-pound golden retriever named Boomer, a member of the Dickenson family in Madison, Connecticut.

On the day that I arrived with our TV crew, cameras running, Boomer bounded out the front door and almost floored me, rearing up on his hind legs to say hello. The Dickensons led the way to the pond in their backyard, and Boomer, who had raced ahead, waited impatiently on the dock. One of the Dickensons threw a large black inflated inner tube out into the lake and, in an instant, Boomer roared off the dock and swam to it.

The cameras rolled and I stood there fascinated as Boomer managed to climb on top of the inner tube by himself, wiggled around until he was perfectly comfortable, and then placed his chin down. He closed his big brown eyes as he floated peacefully around the lake, asleep. He can spend hours this way. Apparently, Boomer learned to do this after watching the Dickensons float in their tubes a few times; one day he tried it himself.

THE WHITE SHEPHERD

After hearing me talk on the air about bringing Spike the sheltie to the office for a week, listener Daniel Russell Ginnetti wrote to me about his white German shepherd, Zoe:

> Zoe was constantly by my side for just short of ten years. She listened to everything that I would say even when the words weren't directed toward her. Her large pointed ears would stand straight up and she would cock her head from side to side and hang on my every syllable. Because of this constant interaction with me and exposure to friends who would also speak to her, she developed, much to my astonishment, an understanding vocabulary of almost two hundred words.
>
> Her time was divided between living in Manhattan on Central Park West, in Newport on the ocean, and in Canterbury, Connecticut, in the country. This exposure to many different people and places, combined with a keen shepherd intelligence, prompted my friends to declare Zoe a "fur-person."
>
> In New York she would stalk squirrels in the park with Isaac Stern's golden retriever, Beverly Sills's springer spaniel, and Shere Hite's 57 Variety.

She was even photographed on several occasions by Andy Warhol. Her portrait is now immortalized in his pet series.

One late spring day, while stalking a squirrel in Central Park, she disappeared. I was frantic. It was an unusually beautiful Saturday afternoon and the park was full of people. My friends and I looked everywhere to no avail. The park rangers, the SPCA, and the local precincts were all notified in case she should turn up. Five and a half hours later I wearily headed up Central Park West trying my best to fight my feelings of defeat. When, there, sitting in front of my building with the doorman was Zoe with a look on her face as if to say, "Where the hell have you been?" All were astonished about how she could find her way out of the park, cross Central Park West, and then find the building.

In Newport, Zoe was famous. She would spend days sailing with us and then, once ashore, she would lie down outside the Candy Store and the Black Pearl and wait patiently no matter how long I was inside. She played with the von Bulows' four blond Labs and teased Doris Duke's guard dogs through the fence.

On her fifth birthday a group of my friends organized a birthday party for Zoe at one of Newport's popular Italian restaurants, Perrini's.

Picture ten reasonably intelligent, well-adjusted adults sitting around a table wearing party hats, singing "Happy Birthday," while the restaurant's owner comes out of the kitchen with a plate of meatballs with lighted candles stuck in each one, placing them in front of Zoe's seat at the head of the table. A verse of "Happy Birthday" was then followed by what had become Zoe's trademark song, "Memories" from *Cats*. She would lift her head up and with a half howl and half wail sing along. The entire restaurant was in hysterics.

Zoe fell victim to Lyme disease. By the time it was diagnosed, treated, and cured, it had already done irreparable damage to her spinal column. Within a short time her back legs became completely paralyzed. Her mind, however, was sharp as ever. She hadn't lost her desire to stalk squirrels, she just couldn't do it without help. She initially showed signs of depression but as soon as she was aware that nothing had changed, and that I would become her back legs, she was back to normal. So I decided I would be there for her just as long as she had the zest for life. I devised a sling to hold up her hindquarters while her front legs were still good and strong enough to carry her one hundred and five pounds.

Zoe lived for a full year like this until Christmas Eve, 1990, when she let me know it was time to go. The vet left me to be alone with Zoe. I sang to her the few lines of "Memories." I haven't been able to listen to that song again without welling up and feeling Zoe's spirit.

CHAPTER TEN

Behind the Scenes

Listeners are sometimes curious about how our call-in show works behind the scenes. I am able to do what I do partly because of the work of many people at the station, including our crew of volunteers.

We affectionately refer to our volunteers as "The Ladies," smart, funny, and resilient women who have spent the past seven years answering calls coming in to our show. They reassure first-time callers and explain to all the rest how to begin once they go on the air. The Ladies have always suggested to me great characters for an episode of the television series *Murder, She Wrote*. Nearly all of them are retired and two spent their careers as secretaries at the FBI.

After handling the phones, the volunteers run down a long corridor to the main studio to hand the engineer a small square of paper with the caller's name written on it; the engineer holds up this paper so that I know the name of the next person on the air. When I tell The Ladies I could eliminate their hallway sprints with a few simple pieces of equipment, they say, "Nah, that wouldn't be any fun."

I always come away wondering if Pat Breuer, Eleanor Devine, Miriam Devine, Gloria Litsky, Marcie McKeon, Libby Patton, and Marian Roy have any idea of how much they have come to mean to me. (Carmel Sullivan and John Horsey have just signed on.)

DIANE: MUSIC MEMORIES

It is close to airtime and I am sitting in the lavender-walled studio with my chair positioned so that I can see through the large glass window into master control, where the show's senior producer, Diane Orson, is coordinating the action. She and I have learned to read each other's faces with precision; with the slightest nod or look from me, Diane will roll with any new idea or change in plans. Anything and everything can happen during a live radio show. I like it that way.

In an age of remarkable technical achievements, many broadcast producers become more obsessed with "perfect sound" than with a show's content, striving for everything according to plan. I like surprise.

We have run fifty-foot cables out the downtown studio door so that I could barbecue ribs on the sidewalk as rush-hour traffic whizzed by.

We have helped free a battered woman serving a life sentence in prison, and we have held a slide show on the air. (I described what was interesting about what was being shown.)

At the suggestion of my friend Bob Gregson, we once positioned a desk and phone on the downtown sidewalk in the middle of huge lunchtime crowds, posting a printed sign that said THE COMPLAINT DEPARTMENT IS OPEN. As hoped, workers and shoppers paused to eyeball us and then sat down, rattling off their personal complaints.

Producing many of these shows with me, Diane Orson has been talented, generous, and kind. No one could be more grateful than I am for her contribution over seven years. (As I write this, she is about to take maternity leave for her second child, Max. And I am lucky once again to have a talented jazz composer, Rex Cadwallader, who created the show theme music, now making his special contribution to the show.)

Considering Diane's background as a classical violinist, it is not surprising that she and I have had some of our most interesting collaborations about music. I couldn't wait to tell her about an idea that came to me, as many do, while riding to work in the car.

I was cruising down Interstate 95, listening to fifties and sixties tunes on the radio, when I began thinking about the powerful memories music can evoke. By the time I reached our New Haven studio, I had a plan. Diane and I would each play the music we especially like on the air, telling our own stories about what it helped us remember, and then invite listeners to do the same about their own "memory music."

With a Beatles song on the turntable the first time we tried it, Diane told listeners what it felt like to play at an international music event in Bulgaria, where none of the musicians spoke the same language. One evening, after a week of hand signals and attempts at communication, the orchestra members gathered together in a big room and one of the musicians began strumming a Beatles tune on the guitar. Every musician began singing along in English. The Beatles were an international language.

We opened the phone lines to callers and the lines were continually jammed.

FINALLY HUMAN

A man named Earl told us in a sweet voice that the sixties hit "Runaway" brings back memories of 1961 when he was in navy boot camp and feeling alone. "You're with a bunch of somewhat frightened young men, and there's no time for the radio or newspapers so you don't know what the world is like anymore. And you're treated as though you're not very important. One Saturday I was assigned to a desk watch from about two to six in the morning at regimental headquarters, so I went over, and there was this old man who'd been in the navy for twenty years. He said, 'Hi, Earl, you sit here and there's some coffee and the newspaper.' It was the first time in five weeks that I'd been treated like a human being. I sat down and answered the telephone the way I was supposed to, and the radio was on. 'Runaway' was the number one song in the country and it played about four times during my watch. Periodically, the old sailor would come out and say, 'How you doin', Earl?' When watch was over, I finished up my coffee and said good-bye to the old fellow, and as I walked out of the building the sun was coming up and people were marching to chow, and for the first time I said to myself, I'm in the navy. I can live with this. And to this day, every time 'Runaway' comes on the radio, I remember being nineteen years old."

A BRIEF DUET

Diane recalled a story about the way music can say things for you. "It was my first crush in high school. We sat next to each other in the youth orchestra in Providence. He was Chinese, and I really wanted to date him. Finally, at one point, my father very kindly sat down and explained that this boy came from a strict family, probably was going to only go out with Chinese girls, and that even though he might really like me, he would never be able to ask me out. That was true. I could practically sense it from this boy, though we never talked about it. We had the opportunity to play a piece together, the Christmas Concerto by Corelli. If you listen very closely, you'll hear that two violins are talking back and forth to each other. And to me, it always symbolized the words that we could never say."

INNER GEOGRAPHY

Yale University English professor and author Wayne Koestenbaum joined me in the studio for a music memory show and brought along some of his favorite classical records. What seemed to stir listeners most was his remark about old recordings: "People who are gone are still here in music."

The first call came from Ethel, who remembered a Sunday afternoon with her husband, George, six years ago. "Although George didn't have a musical ear, there were two classical pieces he learned to enjoy and hum in his off-key way, the opening movement of the Mozart G Minor Symphony and the finale of the Sibelius Second Symphony. I put them both on that afternoon while he was in the house working and it was actually the last thing I was able to do for him because he died of a sudden heart attack that night. I couldn't hear those pieces for about a year, but now when I listen I hear him humming. He's with me."

Wayne told a story about listening to opera singer Anna Moffo on a 1964 recording. "I had just moved to Baltimore, unpacked nothing but my stereo and a sleeping bag. I put on an aria from *Rigoletto*. Moffo's uniquely voluptuous voice filled an apartment and a life I didn't yet know. Twenty years later, the recording still makes me feel the future. And listening to her voice here, I think, language is amazing, isn't it? That words can be sung in such a way that they become so tender; how the sound travels through her throat. . . . I don't know if everyone has the same experience I do, of being ravished by beauty."

I asked Wayne if he felt Moffo had properly christened the apartment. "The apartment wasn't worth it, really, but it did christen a decade of coming out as a gay person and coming into expressivity as a way of life. I decided I would not be shut in but would open my mouth, defiantly, as often as possible."

THANKS, HUGO

Rosemarie pictured her late husband, Hugo, who played the piano beautifully. "I was driving one night through a bad storm, with big trucks all around me on Route 91. I said to myself, 'Oh, Hugo, please bring me home safely,' and when I turned on the radio they were playing, of all things, these Viennese pieces my husband played. And they went on until I reached the traffic circle near my home. I felt there was warmth and protection around me."

BENCHMARK OF THE SPIRIT

*W*hile working for a year as a producer on the show, my friend Bill Storandt, a great writer, sent me a memo about one of his own music experiences, and I read it to my listeners:

When I was the percussion instructor at the University of Vermont, the music department chairman asked me to be part of a faculty jury to listen to a student who was applying to be a music major. That student, Dennis Lampher, had severe congenital deformities of his hands and arms, and he was applying as a percussionist. The chairman's plan was that we would go through the motions of auditioning him, but would, of course, deny his application because it was obvious he could never perform at an adequate level to fulfill the requirements, including a senior recital, for graduation. I agreed with this premise. At the audition, Dennis played only the snare drum and this eased my conscience since he'd have to learn tympani and mallet instruments like the vibraphone and xylophone from scratch in order to meet the definition of percussionist required for graduation. And his snare drum playing was a bit shaky at best, though admittedly quite proficient given his disabilities. So he was denied admission.

A year later he turned up at Johnson State College, also in Vermont, where I taught percussion, but Johnson State had an open admissions policy. Any Vermont high school graduate could attend and declare any major, so there was no way to keep him out. This made me very uncomfortable. I believed it was irresponsible of the school to let students like this believe there was any chance they could make a living in the real world with these kinds of strikes against them; plus, I thought he'd be bitter toward me for my part in his rejection at the University of Vermont. I knew we had to have a talk. I tried to be unsparingly clear with him about the harshness and the competitiveness of the professional world. He listened respectfully until I ran out of things to say, and then he said he wanted to go ahead. No anger, no bitterness, no heroism, just "let's get on with it." Realizing I hadn't budged him, I said, "Well, all right, let's make a deal. I'll teach you for a year on the vibraphone. We'll give this our best shot. We'll be as ingenious as we can about trying to figure out ways to help you play, but after a year we'll have another talk, and if it still looks impossible, we'll give it up." He agreed so we set to work. We devised ways to use rubber bands to enable him to hold the mallets and experimented with different kinds of strokes and angles of attack, sort of reengineering the whole approach to the instrument. He practiced for hours every day, never complained or showed any frustration with his overall situation, just with his inability to hit that A flat on the third beat. Meanwhile, his interest in mathematics was leading him into deeper studies, and he eventually became a double major in math and music. His skills developed to the point where the mere acrobatics of hitting the right notes could give way to musical interpretation. He soaked up every nuance and rapidly demonstrated a real gift for musical playing, a talent often lacking in students with much more facility. He continued playing drum set as well, at one point playing with a country western band and later performing with the jazz ensemble, which I conducted. In his senior year, he performed a senior recital including Bach, Telemann, and Bartók on the vibraphone. Needless to say, I was a blubbering mess, but, as usual, there was no drama about it on his part; he just wanted to get the job done. He searched for a music teaching job in Vermont after graduation for a couple of years, but the extremely small pool of jobs didn't turn up any vacancies. He was born and raised in Vermont. No thought was ever given to leaving the state, so he finally had to settle for teaching calculus and advanced algebra, which I believe he is still doing. He's married to a writer and he has a baby daughter. On the printed program for his senior recital, he dedicated the event to me for believing in him, or some such phrase. In fact, his no-nonsense, no-excuse belief in himself has stood in my experience ever since as a benchmark for the potential of the human spirit.

CHAPTER ELEVEN

Belief

*T*he first year I was in college, I admitted that I wasn't sure how to study, and one of my best friends, Tom Chauvin, who was in my class, sat with me every other night for a year so that I could follow what he did. From another campus across state, our mutual friend Dee (whom Tom eventually married) would call us both every night and cheer us on.

It was touching to hear the stories my listeners told when I asked them what effect it had on their lives to know someone believed in them at an important time. Larry began with a memory of selflessness.

HE WAS SOMETHING

"*I*'d like to tell you about a fella, Jimmy, that I met working in New York at this button company when I was sixteen. My father was an alcoholic and I was just better off on the streets. At the company, I was a messenger. Jimmy noticed that I was getting kind of scruffy looking because I wasn't bathing. He said I was starting to smell and what was my problem? I explained that I left home. It was winter in 1966 and you could get into the tenements in Brooklyn and sleep in the boiler room on cardboard; that's what I did. I continued school for a while but I quit, so Jimmy offered to help me out. He said, 'You really need a better place to stay.' He took me to Flushing, Queens, which is a white, middle-class neighborhood. Jimmy, by the way, is black and I'm white. I thought it was an extraordinary thing for a black person to do for a white person in the mid-1960s. He took me to the YMCA, where you had to be seventeen to stay, and he just stood there pleading with them until, finally, they gave me a room. We walked outside and I said, 'Jimmy, I don't understand why you took me here.' He said, 'Look, you're a white boy, you can get into this nice neighborhood. I could never do this and I don't know any black kid that could do this, but I could do this for you, so take advantage and good luck with it.' A few months later I went into the army and I never saw Jimmy again. He was something."

HOLD OUT A HAND

I was particularly moved by Kathy, who stopped at a pay phone off the highway to call and tell me, with great urgency in her voice, that a friend can make a difference. "I was twenty years old, estranged from my parents and working in a restaurant. I didn't really feel I had anyone to go to. I was living with an abusive man and no one paid attention except this one young woman. We were waitresses together and she never gave up on me. People would say, 'Oh, all guys are like that,' or, 'Everybody has something.' *It must be me,* was all I could think of. But she kept telling me, 'You don't have to put up with it. You're a beautiful, wonderful person. You're kind, loving. Why do you take it?' The answer was because I was terrified. He was violent and threatened to kill me if I ever left. He killed my dog when I tried to leave. I had to give him all my money. He would ask me how much I made at the end of the night when I came home from working. What the waitress did was a very simple thing. She just kept talking to me, and every time I had an excuse like 'He looks in my wallet' she would say, 'Well, out of your tips every night give me ten dollars. I'll save it for you and when you have enough you can get an apartment.' She went out on a limb when nobody else would and because she really believed in me I got the courage to believe in myself and totally changed my life around. I think she saved my life. Her name was Martha. I really want people out there to know that when they see somebody hurting, it's always worth it to hold out your hand."

TEACHERS GET THROUGH

Almost everyone I know has a story to tell about a teacher who made a difference in their lives. Nina said she doesn't think she would have survived an abusive home life without some of her junior high teachers. "I was getting beat up by my mother before I went to school every day. Jim Martin was running a drama program and he handed over the entire makeup and design program to me. He had given me money to go buy what we needed and my mother accused me of getting the money in other ways, and she made me go back the next day and give it back. He asked me why I was returning it and I just couldn't lie. I told him what she said to me and how she treated me. They phoned the house and told her they knew. It wasn't like it is today where intervention is legal. It was very quiet. I think they made her understand that she stepped over a line she shouldn't have."

When I asked Nina if her mother became less abusive, her answer was chilling: "For a while." Nina asked to publicly thank Mr. Martin, Mr. Gerz, Mr. Wydig, and Mr. Talb, for convincing her that she had a right to be part of the human race.

GREAT EXPECTATIONS

Clarice spoke in an energetic voice and reminded me that what is expected of us can help us fail or succeed. "I grew up in Louisiana Cajun country and went to an all-girl Catholic high school. They taught us business skills so that you could get a job after school. Businesspeople would come to get girls right out of high school because we were so well trained. When I was a sophomore, we had a new nun come in, Sister Alexandria. She was an English teacher and gave us writing assignments. After she'd read them she called me up and she said, 'You can write. Now, when you go to college you're going to have to major in English.' And I said, 'Go to college?' Nobody in that whole area had ever gone to college that I knew of. I ended up going to college and being totally confident that I could write."

I was extremely curious about the reaction of Clarice's family. "They were floored! They had never heard of anything like this. But once they got used to the idea it was like, wow, my daughter is going to college! Then all kinds of girls in our family, of which there were hundreds of people, started going to college. It was like the dam burst."

TRYING TOO HARD

The next voice belonged to a woman with a strong German accent. She spoke of her first year in America, and made me think about my own parents coming to this country for the first time.

"In the 1960s I needed to go back to college because I was alone, raising five boys and two girls. I said, 'I'm going to do this,' and so the first thing I had to do is take an American History course at a junior college. Not knowing how this whole thing was going to work, I came prepared with my little notepad and my very best pen and I sat in class. Professor Reese came into the classroom and he started to talk right away. I had a feeling

I should write down every word which came out of this man's mouth because this is American History and one of the courses that will eventually let me into Connecticut College. I wrote down everything; I was writing and writing, half in German shorthand, half in American, and I was spending hours and hours at home transcribing these notes. This went on for two or three times and then this lovely teacher after class took me aside and he said, 'Why are you writing down every cotton-picking word I say? You write hello when I come into the classroom.' I said, 'I write down everything you say because this is American History and because I'm sure it will be on the test. And if I don't pass this course I will never make it into college.' Meanwhile, my kids would say every time I came home, how did you do on your test? How did you do in class? They really put me on a grill. But this professor gave me the faith. I was ready to throw in the towel and he said, 'Let me make a pact with you. Not everything I say will be on the test. You pay attention but you start writing when I look at you.' "

The teacher followed through with his part of the bargain and Hilda went on to graduate from Connecticut College with high honors.

❧

Joe called me with a story about quitting school when he was just sixteen. "In 1961, when you quit at sixteen in New York City, you had to go to an alternative Continuation High School. Luckily, I found a teacher there who was the first one in my life to tell me I was smarter than I thought. Sixteen year olds in the class were just starting to do multiplication tables and I had already taken algebra. So this teacher convinced me that I was in the wrong place, that these kids were headed for jail and I should get out of there while I had the chance. I went back to regular day school and subsequently went to college, graduated, and became chairman of the Wallingford Board of Education. I always made sure that our alternative program was a strong one. I wish I knew that teacher's name."

CHAPTER TWELVE

Best Good-byes

A friend and I shared a beach house one summer in Stonington, Connecticut, cooking out on a deck overlooking the water and staying up late into the night with visitors, lost in good conversation. When it was time to give up that rental, I wanted somehow to say good-bye to the place. I wandered across the street to the old stone lighthouse where I played ball with the dog and watched the moon on the water.

Then, after the truck had cleared away most of my belongings, I walked from room to room, trying hard to fix on the best memory in each room. I realize now that I was trying to acknowledge to myself what so many of us feel when we say good-bye—something important happened here.

And so with this in mind, I was immediately interested in an idea from my frequent collaborator Bruce Clements. Bruce suggested that we ask listeners for stories about their best good-byes.

HE COULD LET HER GO

*T*he first voice we heard—and the most memorable —belonged to an older Swiss woman, who wanted to talk about how important it can be to assist someone else in saying good-bye. "I helped my father say good-bye to my mother when she died at home. The nurse came to me and asked if I couldn't do something because my father had fallen in love again with my mother and he couldn't let her body go. I went in and watched and after a while I put my arm around my father and said, 'You know what we can do? Maybe we'll pick the most beautiful begonias in the garden because Mother loved big begonias.' 'Yes!' he said, and we went outside to look. When he found what he was looking for, he said, 'That's the one,' picking a big red-orange flower with yellow petals. Then we went in and Father took the flower in his hand and put it in the casket next to her. And now he could let her go. This was beautiful, I will tell you. I saw he wanted to express his love once more, and how do you do that? I think of it when I see begonias."

CARING FOR THE SOUL

*I*t was clear from Ellen's story that she was used to success and worked hard all her life for it. She told us that at a very young age she was appointed an assistant professor of English literature and published her first book while at one of the finest universities in the United States. She was one of only seven women on a faculty of ninety men. I had the sense when Ellen explained her decision that she meant to encourage others to take their dreams seriously. "Without any experience I resigned and gave up prestige in order to paint. It was a life-or-death situation in terms of my spirit and my soul. I decided to be very private at first. I would wake up at three a.m. in terror asking, what have I done, what have I given up? But you pursue your passion because you know it really is a matter of life and death. I'm pleased to say now that I've had two shows on Fifty-seventh Street in New York. I've shown in Chicago, Los Angeles, and San Francisco. I cannot say how thankful I feel. I did not choose painting to be a success, I chose it because I had to be silent, I had to give up language. I had to say good-bye to the field in which I was excellent in order to start a journey that would take me someplace new."

ALWAYS WAVING

*W*hen we heard the story Carolyn told about her dad, it was clear that he is a man worth knowing. "My best good-bye was part of a ritual that started when I was six years old. My brothers and sisters and I would line up in this one window every day and wave good-bye to my dad when he left to go to work. I guess we appreciated that he drove a long way every day and earned the money for our family. This went on for many years, and twenty years later we had all moved out of the house except for my older sister. She says she woke up one morning and happened to be walking by that same picture window, rubbing her eyes and looking out, and she saw my dad, who had the car in that reverse position ready to shift to drive. And he looked up at the window and their eyes met and she waved enthusiastically, and he was already waving. I guess it had been a ritual for so long my dad looked up every day just in case."

NOT JUST ANY CAR

My own father and I did not get a chance to see each other much when I was growing up, but one of the clearest memories I have is of him coming by to pick me up one Sunday morning. We went for a drive in his 1940s gray Plymouth and I remember being thrilled when he said I could name the car. I called it Seagull.

On my show, a listener named Sally made me understand that a car can almost become a member of the family. "We said good-bye to our family car, a 1968 Plymouth Fury we got when I was three and didn't get rid of until I was twenty-one. We all learned to drive in it and we used to take my grandmother for Sunday drives in it. When it was time to take the car away, my brother made arrangements to not be here. Even though the car hadn't been started for months, it started right up on that last day. My mother was cooking at the stove and my father took pictures as they towed it out of the driveway. I sat there and told my mother all the funny things we did in it, and she pretended she was very busy cooking; then she cried and we all cried."

CHAPTER THIRTEEN

Forgiveness

Many years ago, I mentioned to our radio psychologist, Dr. Nancy Horn, that one of my goals was never to be jealous of anyone again. Only kindness must have kept her from laughing. I remember this because Bruce Clements and I decided to look at what it takes to be able to truly forgive someone. Appreciating that wanting to forgive is separate from being ready to forgive, Bruce and I opened the show by saying that forgiving is more like a state of grace, and that, ironically, all either party can do is wait for its arrival.

WHAT IT TAKES

The most important call we received was from a man who identified himself as an African American schoolteacher from Long Island. Jay's voice was soft but assured; I guessed him to be in his late forties. "I was raised in a small community, East Hampton, and being a person of color, we had a lot of injustices happening to us all the

time. I was one of four children, the son who didn't live
up to his father's expectations. I wasn't an athlete and I
didn't have many of the interests he had. So, I got my
food and shelter but there was a distance between us for
most of my life. But then my father had a stroke and got
really sick. We took care of him at home, my brothers
and me and my mother, but I was really the one who
took care of him if he, you know, messed the bed. He'd
seen me take care of my grandmother and grandfather
the same way.

"We had to put him in a nursing home the last few
months of his life and during that time I became closer
to him. I went to the nursing home one day and he had
messed the bed. I never talked about messing the bed, I
used to say, Dad, I've got to straighten out the bed. I
would never expose him; I was very aware of letting him
hold on to his dignity. I would cry all the way to the
nursing home and then cry all the way back. One day,
my father said to me, 'You know, son, I feel so badly for
you because when friends or relatives we hadn't seen
would come by, we would introduce all your brothers
and you would be the last one we would introduce. We'd
say about one brother, oh, he's a great athlete; the other
one's got such drive he's an Eagle Scout; the other one's
a good musician.'

"And, then they would get to me and they would
always pause and say, well, he's a kind person, and they'd
chuckle."

I asked Jay if his father ever said he was sorry, and he

told me about their last days together. "Two weeks before he died, my father let me know he had something to say to me. I had just cleaned up his bed when he said, 'You know, we always used to make a joke about your kindness because you weren't what we wanted. You were everything but. You were too sensitive, always worrying about whether there were flowers on the table. You were always worried about someone else and putting someone else first. We wanted to toughen you up and make you deal with the world because we're of color and we're faced with injustice all the time. I just want to tell you that we laughed about your kindness, but for the last few years I've gotten quite a lot of mileage out of your kindness. I wish I hadn't taken you so lightly for so long.' There was a tear coming down his cheek when he said this; he died two weeks later at age fifty. And when he died, I have to tell you that I enjoyed his funeral. I was relaxed and comfortable because I had come to peace with him that day. I didn't forget the injustice, but I can now see all the other good things."

A SAVING GRACE

Not long after our show on forgiveness, producer Diane Orson walked into my office with a letter and said, "This one is really something."

I got up, closed the door, and pulled out the neatly typed pages Diane had handed me. It must have taken a fair amount of courage to write and send this letter. It's another example that one day, often without warning, the ice finally cracks and melts, and all you can do is feel surprise.

Dear Ms. Middleton:

What has finally spurred me to action is your recent program on forgiveness. A good many things have happened to me in the past seventy years, forty of them spent in Southeast Asia, Africa, and other places around the world. But one of the most momentous events has to do with something bad that someone did to me. Eight years ago, my youngest daughter, twenty years old, was killed in a car accident. Her boyfriend, who was driving, was fooling around with a friend driving another car, with the result that my daughter's car was hit broadside by an oncoming truck, killing her instantly and seriously injuring her boyfriend.

The telephone news was as numbing as it was unexpected, and the emotions all hit me together. As the numbness and refusal to believe began to subside, anger took their place. Then another momentous event began to have an effect. Thirteen years ago I was given the gift of changing from being a desperately sick active alcoholic to an alcoholic who hasn't had a drink from then until now.

Alcoholics Anonymous has taught me about

not trying to change things I can't, about acceptance of other people's actions, and of a nonjudg-
mental view of them. Thanks to this teaching, I
was able to realize that anger toward my daughter's
boyfriend was not only unjustified, but would
very quickly tear me apart. I think it was this
realization that made it possible for me to survive the weeks and months after my daughter's
death.

Survive was about all I was able to do for a
while, but in time I became very anxious to get
in touch with my daughter's boyfriend. It didn't
happen easily. It took me five years to be able to
write to him, but when I did, the rewards for me
were immense. I am enclosing a copy of the letter
I wrote (to Mike), hoping that something in it
may be of help to someone else.

Trying to imagine what he could possibly say, I unfolded the next letter.

Dear Mike,
    Like many people I know, I am something of
a procrastinator, but to put off writing a letter for
over five years is a record, even for me. I have
wanted to get in touch with you since the moment I heard about Jeanne's death, and have found
myself unable to do it for reasons that have
changed as time has gone by.

Right after the accident, of course, you were in no shape to communicate, even if I had gotten in touch with you. I wanted to, though, was concerned about you, kept in touch with your progress through a few acquaintances, and was glad when I learned that you were out of the hospital and apparently on the mend. Joan [another daughter who knew Mike], too, was concerned about you. Perhaps you didn't know that she sent you flowers during the first days you were in the hospital. During that time I hoped that your parents might get in touch with us, though I didn't really expect it. It would have been a tough thing for them to do.

Jeanne's death changed our lives, as you can imagine, and although it seems easier to handle now than it was five years ago, the pain when it hits is just as great as ever and undoubtedly always will be. When something this powerful happens I think we try our best to do something about it, even though we realize that there is nothing we can do. My writing to you is the one thing I haven't done, so I'm doing it now. I have a feeling that it may close the circle of events, and that it may be helpful to both of us.

Among many emotions I felt when I got the phone call about Jeanne, some three hours after the accident, was anger, but I didn't really know what or who I was angry at. Some of my friends seemed to think I should be angry at you as the driver of the car, and for a while I was, but I soon realized that it wasn't that simple. My real anger was at the situation, that I couldn't do anything to change it, and that was a very destructive feeling. So much so, in fact, that I soon realized that wherever the fault lay, I could tear myself apart by having feelings of anger and vengeance, and thank God, I was able to get rid of them pretty quickly.

This letter will make sense only if I say what I think; and what I think is that you made a mistake and showed poor judgment. I find myself unable to blame you for this, even though the results were devastating to me. I have made mistakes and have used bad judgment (a number of times in connection with driving a car) and I don't feel I am in a position to condemn others who have done similar things. I didn't make my mistakes on purpose or through malice, and neither did you. Joan says you are a nice guy. Jeanne obviously thought so, and I'm sure I would too, if I knew you.

I'd like to hear from you, Mike, if you feel like writing or phoning. In any case, I feel that this letter makes a long-delayed connection that can do us both good.

I phoned the Rhode Island man who wrote these letters to thank him and tell him how much his words meant to me. He explained that it had taken him five years to write to Mike because he was afraid. Mike, after receiving this letter, had phoned from a couple of thousand miles away and they talked for half an hour. The young man ended the call by saying, "I'm glad you don't hate me."

The Rhode Island man told me that some of his friends have praised him for his action, calling him big-hearted, forgiving, and broad-minded, but he thinks the compliments don't apply at all. "After hearing from the young man," he explained, "I felt better than I had at any time since my daughter had been killed. I hope he did, too, but I know what a saving grace it was for me."

CHAPTER FOURTEEN

Parents and Their Children

Is there any relationship more rich and complex than the one between a parent and child? I have read and loved stories about the reality of family lives from Dorothy Allison, Richard Bausch, Amy Bloom, Blanche Boyd, Fannie Flagg, and Josephine Humphries. And I have heard terrific and poignant stories from my listeners about their own families.

FOR THE LOVE OF PETE

When I sit in my chair and watch the strip of green phone lights flashing, I sometimes think to myself, what if we miss an important story because the lines are full? In fact, we did miss out on Pete Gottlieb's story one busy afternoon. Luckily, Pete and I were on a harbor cruise a few weeks later, and he introduced himself to me. He said he couldn't get through to tell me about his son, and he promised to send me a note. He wrote,

Dear Faith,

Some years ago my twenty-year-old son suggested one Friday night that we meet for a drink at his favorite alumni hangout. We met early, seven o'clock, and promptly picked out perfect stools on the fifty-yard line of this horseshoe-shaped bar.

As we talked boy talk, man talk, life, school, politics, the bar crowd mushroomed with literally hundreds of well-wishers and back-slapping pals of all sizes and shapes. I was so proud of my son's popularity and, of course, was introduced to the growing gang of admirers as a buddy. As the din grew louder with each beer salute, my son gently placed his arm around my shoulder, pulled me close, and whispered in my ear, "Is there anyone else here?"

I have never felt so loved in my life—never!

PARENTS FOR 365 DAYS

Just when Patricia had adjusted to the idea that she and her husband could not conceive a child, life took an interesting turn. "One morning the school psychologist asked to see me and she mentioned that there were two little boys who were in a crisis home situation and had to be removed immediately. We were asked to intervene and take these boys for two weeks. I went home and talked to my husband and we agreed we would do it. The boys were seven and nine years old. At the end of the two weeks, we had this decision to make; would we continue to do this for a year, or should we tell them we weren't ready. So we did it and we put an awful lot into it, knowing it was going to be just a year. I am so grateful that I had this experience, that I could see what it was like to be a parent for an entire year. The boys used to tell their friends, when they introduced me to new people, 'This is my mom for a year.' "

I learned from Patricia that the boys were reunited with two other siblings and they all live with their grandparents; it didn't work out with their own parents. Patricia and her husband are still in touch and they see the boys frequently.

NOTICING COURAGE

I can still hear the way Mary Ellen told me about her children. She spoke of them with such respect. "My children inspire me every day. My six-year-old son has cystic fibrosis, which means once a year he's in the hospital for two weeks, and he has to endure getting repeated, painful IVs. He's very little, so it can be hard to find the right spot. Watching him is amazing. When he finds out that an IV is failing and he will need another one, you can see the fear in his face and then watch him work to overcome it. It can be hard; he might be brought into another room, surrounded by four people he knows are going to hold him down. Given time, he will find the strength within himself to stay still despite the pain. I also have an older daughter who amazes me with her quiet strength. When my son was smaller, I would spend virtually all my time at the hospital, and often my daughter would have to go somewhere for weeks at a time. She was five years old when my son was diagnosed, and from then until now she has stood there and told me everything will be okay. It's astounding. People have to learn to respect what children are capable of."

A SON SAYS HE IS BLESSED

I keep up an occasional correspondence with a listener I met on the air. Jeremy is probably in his early twenties. I don't know how to convey the kindness in his voice or how touched I was by his honesty about himself. "About ten years ago, I became mentally ill, and I had a lot of difficulties with my folks. They didn't understand me at all and I didn't really understand them. But they began attending self-help support groups for the families of the mentally ill and they changed dramatically. They are in many ways more understanding and supportive than any doctor I've had, and I've had some good doctors. It's funny, I almost don't recognize my parents. They surprise me, they aren't aloof, they pay attention, and they're so gentle. When I first left school ten years ago, I said the most horrible things to them; I was out of control. Sometimes I wish I could go back and undo that, so I just thought I'd call you and say what they've done is incredible. We're very close now."

I asked Jeremy if he thought his parents realized it was his illness doing most of the talking in those years. "I think they understand that my illness was talking then better than I do; I keep blaming myself and asking myself, 'How could I have done that?' My therapist helps me get perspective but that's an ongoing process that takes years."

I said, "I bet they don't get frightened like they used to," and Jeremy answered, "That's the biggest change, in some ways. As I've gotten to know them better, and they've learned that they can talk about their feelings, I've come to realize that a lot of the problems we had were about communication. I just feel so blessed."

CHAPTER FIFTEEN

Cheers for Single Parents

I listen to politicians making pronouncements about the gloom of single-parent families and I think how much they miss the point. Instead of condemning these families, I wonder why some of our leaders don't skip the posturing and offer these families the support and resources that they deserve. Life is harder and sometimes impossible when you're raising your kids by yourself, and yet single-parent families at times overflow with love and caring, just as two-parent families do.

What I try to offer listeners who are single parents is encouragement, because I believe that what many of these women and men accomplish with fewer resources is phenomenal. When I opened the phones to give these parents a chance to tell us about their own loving moments, they responded with a roar.

Margaret's life experience does not match the nuclear-family fantasies of some in Congress, but if you ask me, we should all be so lucky. "When I was five years old, I was very ill with polio before they had a polio vaccine. I spent quite a long time in the hospital in an iron lung, and then a year with a therapist to learn how to walk and do everything all over again. Lying inside that iron lung, which breathed for me, had a profound effect on my life in many ways. The thought of an airplane as an iron lung kept me from flying for fifteen years. Both my parents are dead now, but my mother was someone who praised us for who we were and what we did as long as we were trying our best. Neither of my parents could visit me while I was in quarantine, but I can remember her always sending me notes that said, 'You will get better. You were put here for a reason and you're going to get better.' Well, I did; I only had a little bit of a curvature in my spine and some postpolio muscle aches. But as time went on, my mother never even looked at my report cards. She just asked me if I felt I did well, and I would say yes. When I decided I didn't like college and wanted to work, she said, 'If that's what you think you're going to do, I believe in you.' And I did very well. Then I became an alcoholic. I drank until I found out I was pregnant with my first child. I told my mother I wasn't going to drink anymore. She said, 'I believed that you would make up your mind to do what was right for your health and the health of your child when that time came.' My daughter is now twenty years old and I haven't had a drink since then. Then I got breast cancer. I was married and it was not a good marriage; I was alone for most of it except for my girls and my mom. It was a deep cancer so I had to have anesthesia for the biopsy. I woke up and my mom was there. I looked at her and I said, 'I have cancer.' And she said, 'Yes, and you will beat it the same way you beat polio and alcoholism because you were meant to be here for a reason.' I had chemo and radiation. And here I am five years later, divorced, with two daughters who are amazing. I've tried to raise them the same way my mom raised me. I'm watching these girls turn into very strong, goal-oriented women who freely discuss any feelings and concerns they have."

DAD'S LEGACY

Maryann and Karen lost their husbands and struggled to keep their families intact, but the challenge did not mean there was an absence of love. Maryann said, "My husband was killed in an explosion on the job five years ago and I finally settled the lawsuit. I had promised my kids that when we settled we would go to Disneyland. We did, we spent a week there, just the three of us. I really felt like I was one of the few single parents down there; it just seemed everywhere we turned we saw Mom, Dad, and two kids. Maybe we didn't have anybody else there for us and yet we had the most wonderful week. We were with each other twenty-four hours a day, and we just enjoyed each other. It was like my husband was sending us to Disneyland."

ROGER NEEDS US

*K*aren also lost her husband to a brain tumor ten years ago, leaving her to care for three teenagers. "It happened on the last day of my internship in medicine. I was on call and had these three grieving children and my own grief. I called because you asked what made us a family. For us it was my oldest child, Roger, who is basically disabled with learning disabilities. The love of the other two children for him has been inspiring to me. Roger needs us and that has made us a unit. Roger is in Special Olympics, and the whole family troops down to watch him play tennis. We sit in the hot sun on bleachers; there aren't usually too many people there, and we yell our heads off for Roger, who looks like a real tennis player. We know, 'This is us, our family, and we're together.' Dad was a tennis player and he would have been so proud of us. We hug Roger when it's over and take him out to dinner."

ULTIMATE LOVE

*A*fter getting a call from a friend inviting her for a week's vacation in Florida, Stephanie, a single parent for eleven years, thought she shouldn't go, though she had just spent the last year caring for her dying father. "Then my daughter told me there was a mother-daughter dinner during the time I planned to be away. I was going to cancel my trip but she climbed into my lap and said, 'No,

Mom, I want you to go. Auntie will take me.' It was ultimate love. Here was a child thinking that Mommy had a really bad year and really needed to get away for five days. And when I got off the plane at the end of vacation, she was standing there at the airport with a single rose in her hand, her eyes all filled with tears because Mom was home."

THEIR OWN LITTLE UNIT

I love the stories two callers told about the kinds of moments that happen in many families but are hard to explain. Dana said, "I'm twenty-two and a full-time college student, so my two-year-old daughter and I get involved in our routine; we don't have much time to just enjoy ourselves. Please don't laugh at me when I say this. One day last fall, on a perfect seventy-degree day, I had an afternoon off from school, and the two of us went out back to the big school field. There were kids playing in the field. We just sat there and kind of became one. She was in my lap, and then our cat came over and sat down right next to me. It was our own little unit. I never felt so whole."

FOREVER AND EVER

*M*arge would understand. She said, "A month ago on one of those rare spring days, I picked my daughter up from school and we had a cozy time together. We had a lovely evening picnic on the lawn. When I put her to bed, she burst into tears, and I said, 'Hey, what's the matter here?' And she said, 'Today was perfect and I don't ever want anything to change. I want to be five and a quarter years old forever and you stay exactly the way you are forever.' I was astounded by it. It gave us the chance to talk about the nature of change, and how great it is when perfect days come to us, and that we would have more perfect days. I was so touched that she knew what a perfect day it had been."

HOMEWORK FAMILY STYLE

I don't think Rose imagined when she became a single parent that she and her children would study together. "I returned to school and one of the nicest things about it is that we all do our homework together. We'll be lying on my bed, and we each have a pillow for our books, and we're either reading or writing. Sometimes we have music on and sometimes we don't. They'll say, 'Can you help me with this?' Or, I'll say, 'Can you help Mommy with this?' It's such a calming, wonderful thing."

JAMIE WINS

*J*ust about every person I know can sympathize with the juggling of schedules and skills that go into raising a family, and yet in the midst of it all there are parents like Janet, who notice and appreciate important qualities in their kids. "I have two children, Megan and Jamie, four years apart, and they're competitive, as many siblings are. A couple of years ago we were staying at a friend's cabin in Maine; there was nobody else there and we were truly isolated. We played cards together, and my son, Jamie, usually never wins. But on this evening the little guy actually started to win. My daughter, Megan, and I were absolutely rejoicing. We both gave him big hugs and kisses."

A SON WHO CARED

The last thing Theresa expected was that her son would show his love for her the way he did. "A long time ago, when my little boy was seven, he heard a school doctor say that for every cigarette you smoke you lose one minute of your life. He ran home and asked me how many cigarettes I had smoked and there were tears in his eyes. 'I don't know,' I said to him, 'but I can do something that will make both of us happy.' We burned up the cigarettes, and I never smoked again. I didn't want to give my little son any more problems. He's forty now and he himself never smoked. I understood that he was telling me, 'I love you, Mom, I need you, don't kill yourself.' "

GOD BLESS

Cruising up and down the radio dial, as most of us do, Gloria stopped when she heard my voice asking single parents to call in. "I was so elated that you wanted these stories. All the moments of my life with my son have been precious. He's twenty-nine now, and to think that I had no intentions of having him; it was like 'Pop Goes the Weasel' when I was in junior college. I never went on welfare, not that I have anything against welfare. I never shacked up with a man. It was God who helped me raise my son. I taught my boy how to meditate on the scriptures for fifteen minutes every day before he went to school. He would go to his room and I would go to mine for those fifteen minutes, and even in that we were learning to be independent of one another. Today, we have so much love. We're just so close, and he treats me as if he was still three years old. You know how some young men get old and don't want to be seen kissing in public? My boy says, 'Hey, Mommy!' and he kisses me in public. God bless you for having a program for a single parent."

CHAPTER SIXTEEN

Shows from Home

Just like that, everything was different. One minute, I was on my way to a Thanksgiving weekend celebration on Cape Cod, and the next minute I was home in bed in agonizing pain. An impatient driver rammed the rear of our car and the impact tore all the muscles in my lower back.

I learned I would spend four to six months alternating between bed, to rest the injured muscles, and physical therapy, to rebuild the injured tissue. After a week of lying there bewildered, I suddenly thought, why not broadcast my show from home? I believed listeners would be interested in hearing the expected and unexpected sounds of daily living on the air, and that it could provide the kind of delightful spontaneity that makes radio come alive. I now realize that what motivated me motivates many seriously disabled people; I couldn't move in the same way I used to, but I knew I could do meaningful work.

Appearing at my door the next morning with his bag of equipment, one of my trusted colleagues, Eugene

Amatruda, rigged up a system that enabled me to talk into a microphone from the couch; my voice was fed directly into the telephone line, which connected me with our studio in New Haven. The guests sat where they always did in the New Haven studio, and talked with me a half-hour drive away, at home.

I could not have pulled this off without The Ladies volunteer team, mainly because I was frequently in the kind of pain that would almost make me pass out. The volunteers took turns sitting next to me each day, signaling when callers were on the line, and when to take our breaks for news and weather. They brought home-cooked meals and offered encouragement, and I will always be indebted to them for their kindness.

While I lay there thinking about what my first show from home should be about, a friend suggested that I ask listeners how they coped with the unexpected in their own lives.

Having made the painful transition from bed to the living room, I opened that first show by telling listeners about the accident. (In the coming weeks, people I had never met called me or sent letters of encouragement, and little presents: what a lift when I needed it most.) Then I said, "I'm stretched out here on the pink sofa; I can do very little by myself. Some days I accept it, some days it makes me mad. Today, I ask you to tell me about a time in your life when you were helpless physically or emotionally. How did you cope? What was most helpful in getting you through it?"

While callers were getting on the line, I interviewed two people who know something about coping. At the time of our conversation, I barely knew Edder Bennett, who has since become a close friend; he was about to graduate from Yale Law School.

When I asked him to explain to listeners what rendered him helpless, Edder said, "I don't actually consider myself helpless, although dependent in some ways I certainly am. I broke my neck in a diving accident fourteen years ago. I'm a C5-6 quadriplegic, meaning I'm paralyzed. There are many things that I can't do for myself, that I have to ask other people to do for me. For the first year or two after the accident, there were times when I had acute feelings of helplessness, so I know what you mean."

I wondered if at first he felt depressed and furious. "I remember not being able to feed or dress myself. I was in a Stryker frame in an uncomfortable hospital bed. For a while I couldn't move my arms or even breathe by myself; I had a feeding tube. First I was scared, then frustrated and angry, but you don't even know who to be angry at. It took me quite a while to learn what tools were available to get things done, and to redefine what dependence and independence are."

I told Edder that the remarks that were getting to me were "Try to remember what you can be grateful for." I added, "I don't really want to hear it; I'm still shocked that this has happened at all."

When I asked him what he meant about redefining

dependence and independence, he said, "Too often we build our identities around what we do instead of who we are. We look at our accomplishments, résumés, IQs, and the amount of weight we can lift in the world to define who we are. Less frequently do we investigate our own values and the subtler contributions we make to the lives of others and our communities. It was hard for me because in the two years before I broke my neck, I traveled around the world alone and worked for a U.S. senator in Washington; then I enrolled at Yale. I defined myself by such accomplishments, and suddenly I was putting square pegs in square holes and learning how to use a fork and a telephone. I have discovered since then that it's tempting to invest in ourselves only that which we've accomplished and not that which we believe in, or what we do for others. I think we can move beyond an independence of body to an independence of mind, even of identity."

I told Edder that I felt guilty about being able to recover many physical abilities when he would not.

"But, actually," Ed answered quickly, "I've recovered the physical abilities necessary to do the things I love the most in the world, to be a friend, to be someone's partner, a law student. I'm not trying to be Pollyanna; I would like to be able-bodied again; I was once and preferred it."

There was one point that was important to me to get across. I told the listeners, "When I called our station and said I wanted to go on the air from home, everybody jumped in to assist: my friend Blanche, the radio staff, and my sister, Sally, who is sitting right next to me for this first show. Everyone believed in my ability even though I have certain physical limitations. They understand that I still have a contribution I can make. I want to say that I realize more than ever that there are a lot of disabled people in the world who have contributions to make. How can anyone doubt the value of the Americans with Disabilities Act?"

I spoke next with a remarkably talented man, Jack Plummer, then head of the psychology team at Gaylord Hospital in Wallingford, Connecticut. Gaylord is a respected facility for treating people with disabilities and assisting them in functioning in the mainstream. Our exchange went like this:

JACK: I think you've had an intellectual understanding of disability, Faith, and now you're living it. Pain takes a toll on the psyche. I don't think of accepting a disability ever, although "acceptance" is commonly used in the disability community. I think it's asking a lot of anyone to accept a disability; rather, I think of it as adapting to a disability. Why should you accept what just happened to you?

FAITH: What a great thing to say.

JACK: I think one of the worst things anyone could tell someone in your situation is that it could be worse. You don't need someone who is not experiencing a disability at the time to say that things could be worse; that has never been very helpful. As a matter of fact, it can create anger and depression. Your greatest resource now is not your body, it's your mind; the mind is even more powerful than the body. We've only just scratched the surface in understanding how to use our minds in valuable ways. You can feel sorry for yourself as long as you don't do it too long because that's counterproductive. Say to yourself, I can't make my body do very much right now but what can I do mentally? Some people use this opportunity to do some soul-searching and character-building. I have a friend with a spinal cord injury and he says it was a character-building experience but he'd certainly give all that up if he could walk again. I think you may learn a lot about yourself through this experience, but it's really your call as to whether it's worth it or not.

STORIES FROM BRAVE CALLERS

*E*ven I was surprised by the number of callers who had stories to tell about suddenly being rendered helpless, including the first man, Bart, who was at home with his eyes bandaged. "I'm alone now in the house; my wife will be back in an hour or so. It took me three tries to visualize where the numbers are on my telephone to call you now. I was on my way home from Maine when I had a torn retina. Before I knew what was going on an eye doctor had me in a chair and I was going through laser surgery; I've got to be on my back with my eyes closed for a week. I'm a lawyer who has a lot of disabled clients but after this I'm much more appreciative of their situations; this has been excellent sensitivity training."

The next caller, Dina, said she was nervous and that she had never talked publicly about her depression. "It happened fifteen years ago when I was a twenty-year-old college student, and it has become a big part of who I am. I had never experienced such helplessness; I'd go to the grocery store but I couldn't deal with the choices there. I'd open the refrigerator to get something to eat and it was overwhelming. I'd look in the drawers and, well, decisions were just out of the question. I went into a private psychiatric facility and that was upsetting because my family made the decision. I didn't want people to tell me, 'Don't worry; this will pass.' First, I didn't believe it and, second, I needed to be where I was for a while; I just needed to be depressed. I felt like the depression was a physical illness and my body needed time to learn how to fight it off. I want to emphasize that I am in no way saying that if anybody depressed is listening, all you have to do is do what I did and it will go away; it has to happen at the right time for your individual depression. You have to be ready to pull out of it. I decided that I wasn't going to lament the fact that I couldn't feel the way I wanted to. I was always saying, 'I know I should be feeling so much happier, or feeling things more deeply.' I remember the moment of decision, when I said, 'I'm just going to look at what I can feel.' There's an old saying, better to light a single candle than to curse the darkness.

From then on, if someone told me she had a baby, instead of saying, 'God, why don't I feel more excited for her?' I'd say, 'At least I know that I'm supposed to feel excited.' I was focusing on the little glimmer of light. That was when I began to heal and learned to cope. I was angry going through it but I've never once regretted the experience because it opened a whole new door to another aspect of life. It has enabled me to reach out to other people who have experienced similar things and say, 'I know what you're feeling, I really do.' "

I thanked Jack and Dina, and as they signed off, I thought to myself what an unexpected comfort it was to me to be able to talk with such a variety of people who wanted to tell their stories in the hope of offering encouragement to others. Daniel said, "I spent fifteen years in a religious cult in the Boston area, a Bible-based group called The Local Church, which has about ten thousand members in this country. I was totally helpless when I emerged from that because I had no idea of who I was. I had taken on a personality that helped me survive within the group. In such groups, everything is very well defined and all questions are answered for you. So, coming back into the real world was complicated; I'd gone in as a single man, and had come out with a wife and four children. What happened was that I burned out in the cult and then was rejected by the people I'd spent fifteen years with; I lost all of the people I considered my friends, and my means of livelihood. I came out with virtually nothing except, of course, a beautiful family."

I learned later from Daniel, who wrote to me, that he dreamed every night that he'd been shot in the back. What helped him recover was a book, *Combatting Cult Mind Control,* sent to him by another ex-member; he read it and eventually met others who had left and survived.

CHAPTER SEVENTEEN

Living Room

*E*ach day I made my way slowly from the bed to the pink sofa in my living room, where I would stretch out with Spike the sheltie curled up by my feet. I live in a small fishing village in an old Victorian farmhouse that offers me quite a view of Long Island Sound. From this outpost, I would tell the listeners about all that I could see: lobstermen unloading their catch, sea and marsh birds sailing elegantly across the sky, and the sun setting in a blaze of colors. On one show, in fact, I asked listeners to call and tell me what they could see from their own rural or urban windows.

All the shows I did from home were filled with observations of what went on around me. If the mail carrier knocked during the show, or FedEx tossed a box on the porch, I let it all happen naturally. Spike barked when she felt like it; the noisy furnace clicked on and off. "This is what life at home sounds like," I would sometimes say to listeners, especially those who might have been cruising the dial and stayed there, curious. I would describe the living room, filled with the warm light from the table lamps, and let listeners know what was piled on my little desk near the sofa. I talked about the day the Christmas tree lights were turned on, along with the colorful ceramic desktop tree my niece Judy made for me.

I described the afternoons when the sky and the water seemed to turn the same color. We drank hot chocolate on the air, and I joked about the loveliness of my hair, which I was unable to wash for a month.

There were many notes and phone calls from listeners who were enjoying the experience of a cozy show from home; in fact, the *Hartford Courant* published a story by Frank Rizzo, who observed the show in my living room and suggested to me and his readers that I keep doing it that way. One of these days I might do just that.

ACTS OF COURAGE

Much as I loved having the dog at my feet during the show, especially when we could hear her sigh one of those deep sighs that dogs do settling in for a big nap, I started putting good old Spike upstairs in a bedroom while I was on the air. I had to. She would look at me as I talked away into a microphone, thinking that I was talking to her, and she would talk back with a growl, or start winging her rubber cheeseburger around, hoping for a game of catch. It struck me as hilarious that she thought I was having hour-long conversations only with her.

With Spike tucked away upstairs and only barking occasionally at the floorboards to register her opinion, I turned my attention to acts of courage one afternoon close to Christmas. I see people being courageous in so many ways that go unnoticed. Like my friend Bruce Clements says, "It can be courageous even to get up in the morning and face another day."

I talked about the determination I often see in courage—the way we put our heads down and barrel on through even though we are sometimes afraid. Or, I see men with the courage to cry even though they have been raised to believe that showing any vulnerability is a sign of weakness. I can't count the times I see courage in children who are constantly asked to try new things, and they do them even while they are afraid.

I asked the listeners to talk about their own acts of courage, even small ones, and not to think of it as bragging. Diane, the producer, whispered in my earpiece, "We're flooded with calls." Here are just a few of them, starting with a lovely woman, Rosa, who told us about a major decision her son and his girlfriend faced. "Nine years ago, when my son was a seventeen-year-old senior in high school, he and his girlfriend got pregnant. Her mother was adamant that she get an abortion. My son argued and pleaded against this, and then enrolled the help of his dad. My boy said he and his girlfriend wanted this baby desperately, that it was their right to have it. The other mother finally relented and allowed them to get married. My son brought his new six-day-old son to his high school graduation. We said we would stand by him whatever he decided; everyone was against him. All his friends were against him and said it wouldn't last. He had to drop out of track and work two jobs after school to support his family. They lived with us and couldn't get medical coverage anywhere. Her family disowned her. I thought my son was remarkable."

Rosa said that her son was so afraid at times that he would sit there, shaking, saying, "I hope I can handle this; I hope I can do it." His parents would tell him, "We're with you; we'll help you if this is what you want."

Rosa told me that her son has been married nine years. "They always go out as a couple; whatever he does, his wife and children are included. He's a licensed contractor and he goes to school at night to study engineering. They have two sons now. I'm amazed at how firm they were when everyone was against them, and how well they're doing."

I asked Rosa about her own fear. "I was absolutely terrified. My husband is a very macho man, and the night he had to plead with her mother for the life of this child, he was shaking as he spoke. As a parent you ask yourself if you're doing the right thing because you don't know how things will turn out. We were very lucky."

JUST ONE LIFE

Eric has a mental illness but he manages to try to keep his focus on what matters. "I got into a supervised apartment which was good because I had more freedom and counselors to talk with. A lot of times people who don't experience something—it's hard for them to understand. I tried putting myself through college and one semester I even made dean's list, but I had to drop out because my medication wasn't right. Last night I found out I lost my job. But I only have one life to live. This morning I went down to Fellowship, which is a marvelous club for people with psychiatric problems. There are people there in all ranges, like people who just got out of the hospital. I said to myself, 'My life is completely falling apart here.' And then the patients from Connecticut Valley Hospital got there and these people were so sick and they have very little in life. I was thinking, here I am complaining and look how much I have in life. I have my own apartment; my parents left me money; I have a chance in this club to make people happy; I know everybody in the club; I have a place to go to. We sang Christmas carols all afternoon and we each said what we might want for Christmas. I said to everybody, 'We've got to try to be happy for what we do have.' I was inspired by everybody there today; they gave me the courage to go on."

FOOD FOR THE HOMELESS

A caller named Patty told me that she began delivering food to the homeless. "I was living in New York and even though I was afraid to do it, I used to bring food to the homeless on the streets in the middle of the night. I saw them in boxes and on benches and wandering the streets without any clothes on. It was hairy but I brought them soup because these people need some kind of sustenance."

CHAPTER EIGHTEEN

Change

I now realize that several of the shows I did from my living room were about change from a variety of angles—change we expect as well as change that surprises us; how we handle change in a relationship; and what we think we can't live without, only to learn that we can.

I knew of the ideal person to talk about change realistically because he never says it's no big deal. I called a man I admire, Dr. James Comer.

Dr. Comer teaches teachers. A professor of child psychiatry at Yale University and recognized as an outstanding educator worldwide, Dr. Comer and his team have been awarded millions of dollars from the Rockefeller Foundation to continue their groundbreaking work, designing new ways to educate children at risk.

I relish any chance to visit with Dr. Comer, because he remains optimistic about the children he works brilliantly to nourish, and in doing so, he reminds us that children at risk not only can be saved, they deserve to be saved; we have the people and know-how to do it.

The basis of Dr. Comer's work involves long-term cooperation among teachers, students, administrators, and parents. Money helps but, surprisingly, the toughest obstacle Dr. Comer faces in accomplishing his task at hundreds of schools nationwide is fear of change.

He has learned over time that he must first coax, support, reassure, and attend to the specific fears that even the most sophisticated school workers face when they are asked to change what they're secure in doing. When I expressed sympathy for those workers, Dr. Comer quickly agreed, and he began a story about his boat.

"For the longest time I wanted to have a boat," Dr. Comer explained, "and I waited and waited for the day that I could." When it finally arrived and he was ready to launch it near his summer place on Martha's Vineyard, Dr. Comer said he became instantly terrified about how to handle such a big craft. He repeatedly ran aground in shallow water and wrecked several propellers over the summer until, he says, "I didn't want to be within five hundred miles of that boat because it was all fear and mistakes when I was, but over time, making many mistakes, little by little I became adjusted to the demands of the boat. I became pretty decent at running it and now I even enjoy it."

Dr. Comer's story was not lost on me, nor, apparently, on our listeners. When I asked them to tell their own stories about handling change, I was struck by how much they wanted to help prepare others for similar challenges.

TAKE A RISK

Ann decided to stop working for other people and go out on her own. "This was scary for me because my family are all employed in the services, you know, doctors, policemen, and firemen. I was brought up thinking that you had to work for someone to be sure your paycheck would be there, and that you had to have a pension. I had a hard time letting go of the security I had as a social worker; at first I was going to work for someone else again, but when I was shown my office, my heart sank, it just went right to the ground. The next day I looked at an office I could have as a self-employed person and my heart sang, it just jumped out of my chest. After all those months of thinking about it and trying to make the right decision, that's what it all came down to. People had said all along, 'Trust your heart; just let it be whatever it's going to be and the outcome will be in your best interest.' I did just that and now I'm self-employed; I work in collaboration with a small group of people I admire as clinicians."

After hearing from Ann, I realized that there are two kinds of change—the change you have no part in, and the change you decide to bring about. The next set of callers didn't want the changes they faced, and yet they survived them and are perhaps stronger people as a result.

FIGHTING YOUR WAY BACK

As Bettina described surviving traumatic brain injury, she had my attention. "I slipped on some ice and hit my head. Lifestar brought me to Hartford Hospital and I was there for six months, much of the time in a coma. They never thought I would make it. I hope someday they will find a cure for traumatic brain injury but now it cannot be. It changes your entire life. When I came out of the coma and they said traumatic brain injury I didn't even know what it was until they explained that almost half my brain was dead. When I was released from the hospital, my only thought was, 'Why didn't they let me die?' My two biggest problems were and are forgetfulness and speech, but thanks to Easter Seals Rehab I can talk again. After the hospital I was despondent; I have no family and no relatives. In rehab I looked at the others and thought, 'Well, they're young and they have whole brains, nothing will help me.' And then one day it just hit me and I accepted that it was up to me. I said to myself, 'Either one kills oneself or one gets off one's derriere and starts fighting.' Today I'm a volunteer on the seventh floor of Hartford Hospital, where the brain-injured patients are. It takes one to know one."

I remember thinking as I coaxed this story from Bettina that change isn't always a clear-cut decision, and that sometimes the courage to handle it arrives almost like grace.

One September day, I watched a friend's young daughter return from her first day of third grade and talk about what it was like to have a new teacher. It made me thoughtful about how easily children handle constant change, and how much they deserve our compassion when they don't handle it well. I like to say, compare your child's first day with a new teacher to how you feel on the first day with a new boss.

DIVORCE IN SUBURBIA

One caller remembered what it felt like to grow up in what he described as a cozy, white-bread-and-jelly neighborhood called Springdale, where the biggest changes were happening at home. "When I was in sixth grade, I came home on the bus with my friends and we saw heavy equipment at the end of our street in the spot that was our favorite playground. We watched in horror as bulldozers began tearing down everything we loved to build a golf course in our cherished woods. This all took place when I was twelve years old and my parents were divorcing. It hit me hard. I stood there and shouted at the construction workers, who eventually put a wire fence around what was once free to everyone. At one point, the construction people took the trees they cut and built a big bonfire to get rid of them. People from all over the community came out to watch the trees burn and talk about the old days. My childhood was over with a thud.

"It seemed like divorce didn't happen to people that you knew, so it was a shock. I remember the day I tried to convince my father in my twelve-year-old language why he shouldn't divorce my mother, although today I realize that they are each better off. A year later, one of the newspapers interviewed families with single parents and they ran a picture of me with the caption, 'Oh, yes, Bob likes to do the cooking,' as if we had celebrity status. I handled it by immersing myself in what I was interested in at the time, music."

What music gave Bob was a feeling of wonder as he absorbed combinations of sounds. "I make a living as a musician today."

I was touched by Bob's story and frustrated, too, because at the time he spoke, I was reading many newspaper stories about local school boards that were axing school music programs to reduce their budgets. I kept thinking of all the kids who might have used music to discover important things about themselves and others. The next caller, Ron, from Sag Harbor, Long Island, was using his creativity to survive happily.

WHAT GOD GIVES YOU

"*I*'m a contractor, builder, and carpenter who has worked on my own for the last twenty years. I've managed to survive because I've had one well-paying client, a famous movie director, but we had a parting of the ways and it cut my income in half. I had a week of sleepless nights because I'm a divorced father and I'm responsible for myself and another household. I'd been wanting to tap into the more creative side of what I do so I went on a leap of faith, I started building the kind of Adirondack style furniture I like. I get up in the morning and go down to my shop and feel excited about working. For the last two months it has felt like I'm not working, although I've produced twenty pieces of furniture and people are very responsive to it. I haven't sold a lot yet but I've always felt that if you love your work, say, picking up garbage, you can be the best garbage hauler in the world and people will respect you and pay you."

I asked Ron if he faced the possibility that he might fail. "You have to have a belief that God will not give you more than you can carry. You've got to think God would treat you like a daughter or a son, that you are loved and someone wants the best for you. So I continue on hope and give it my best."

HOW RELATIONSHIPS CHANGE

When I asked listeners to talk about change in their personal relationships, I opened the show from my usual spot on the pink sofa, saying, "The wind right now is so strong coming off the water, the whole house is shaking. Can you hear all the wind chimes on the front porch?

The antidote to all this cold and wind is this Christmas tree in the corner of my living room. When all the colored lights are on the tree, and they are right now, I feel reassured somehow.

"It's a call-in show today about how personal relationships endure a dramatic change and go on in spite of it, maybe even improved."

I paused for a moment after giving the phone number, my heart beating fast while I thought about what I would do next if the callers weren't there, when Diane whispered in my headphones, "You've got a full house."

A COMMON PURPOSE

Opening her story, Gloria said challenging experiences can sometimes tell you what your mate is made of. "My husband's mother became very ill just after we were married, and I found it necessary and appropriate to go to the hospital and spend part of each day with her, cheering her up. It went on for a very long time, and I was there for the last minutes of her life. This happened while, at home, I had my retarded brother and a daughter from a previous marriage living with us. I realize now that it proved to my husband what he thought he saw in me when we got married. And I appreciated how loyal and sincere he was to his mother despite his job pressures and all the plans we made for our new marriage. It all brought us together somehow with a common purpose."

FRIENDSHIPS SURVIVE

I marvel at the twists and turns some of my friendships take over time; some grow, others wane and, to my surprise, flourish again. Barbara described something like that. "I've been thinking all day about a friend I've had for thirty-five years. We were total buddies growing up together in Philadelphia. She was a very bright and rebellious girl. The first traumatic incident in our friendship happened when she was sixteen and she ran off to Puerto Rico to get married. I knew she was going to do it and I didn't tell on her, which I wish I had. She had a baby and we stayed in contact but our lives were becoming more separate. We would each express our feelings in Christmas cards. Then she divorced her husband and married a horribly abusive person. I would feel guilty sharing my life with her because my life was so wonderful. Then, this summer, waiting in line for an amusement ride, there she was. We ran to each other and sobbed; we were like two fools for twenty minutes on the boardwalk in Wildwood, New Jersey. I could cry now because I think about her constantly. I got a card from her yesterday saying she cares about me and is thinking of me. I listen to her saying what's bad and I don't tell her what's good in my life. I have all our home movies from 1956 when we were kids and I watch her in them. I ask her sometimes why she won't take a train to see me; she's never gotten her driver's license."

I asked Barbara to consider sending a tape of our radio conversation to her friend.

IN LOVE AGAIN

I heard from two callers, one after another, who adjusted to change by getting in touch with the preciousness of time.

Harriet said, "One of my all-time dearest friends has had a very rough life. She and her husband haven't had much. He's an alcoholic and was never really there. She would get so tired of it and think about leaving but she didn't want to break up the family. A couple of years ago her husband almost died; his liver is shot and the doctor said, 'You can never drink again, and we don't know how long you'll live.' My friend said, 'You know, I've never known him when he wasn't an alcoholic; I don't know the man I'm going to live with.' A few months later she said to me, 'Even though we know he's dying, we're happier than we've ever been.' I think they have fallen in love all over again. She says he's a peach. In a way it is a tragic story, but at least they have cherished every minute of the time they have left."

And Joy said, "In July, my husband and I discovered that he has cancer. Being an extremely private person, he didn't want anyone to know, including our daughter, so I sat down with my husband and I said, 'Doug, look, life is going to go on the way it always has and you're going to have to tell people if you lose all your hair like Telly

Savalas.' We had a very personal talk, as personal as we've ever had in our thirteen years of marriage. I think I convinced him to open up to people and kid about it, to talk about what he's going through. As a result, he has made so many people more comfortable around him. He's a banker and some of his customers will come in and throw their arms around him, saying, 'I hope you get better soon.' Other people joke with him, saying his new hair might come in red and curly. It can be very lonely when your friends won't come near you. Treat a friend or relative with cancer as normally as possible."

A FAMILY'S LOVE

A listener named Jack has my respect for the distance he traveled in adjusting to the changes in his son. I would be proud to call Jack my father. "We had a great change in our family ten years ago when we discovered that my son tried to take his own life because he is gay. At first, of course, I was stunned. I was ignorant and fearful over the suddenly vast difference between my child as I always knew and understood him, and the son he now is. We did express our love for him but the truth is that we didn't really know why we still loved him; yes, I guess that's the best way to say it. What helped us survive the changes was love and a difficult education. I was in the closet myself after I discovered our son is gay. I was afraid to ask about it or even borrow a book about it at the library. I finally opened my own closet door when a pastor friend of mine gave me a study that the Lutheran Church had recently done. It had lots of references in the back and I began reading extensively and going to seminars and joining organizations. My wife and I are now longtime members of a national organization called PFLAG, Parents and Friends of Lesbians and Gays. I've changed from a shy, private military man to being an angry outspoken parent. I forced myself to go public, and this call to you is an expression of that. What saddens me the most is that I have lost my faith because I cannot worship a church or God that could harshly judge someone who is born gay, and that is what my Christian faith does. I am outraged at the moral leadership in our world. I think most of us want to believe that our faith teaches us what is right and wrong. They have failed me and they fail terribly all gay and lesbian people and their families on this issue."

I was curious about the reaction of other family members. "As a family we are not the people we were before. We're much more sensitive and aware of what's important in life. A couple of months ago, my daughter in Arizona called and said she wants to move back East, and she indicated she'd like to become more involved with this issue herself. That almost moved me to tears. Our children initially had religious judgments of our gay son, and they have changed their minds. We're all very close to our son now, and he appreciates the support that he gets. He knows too many families who don't support their gay and lesbian children."

❦

After Jack's phone call, I received a copy of an important letter from one of our listeners, a forty-three-year-old man who had written and sent this letter to a mother that he clearly cherishes.

Dear Mother,

My recent trip home was filled with moments of intense love for you. You're looking well, and your energy seems strong and sure. I'm always moved by your devotion to kindness, by your concern for the happiness and well-being of your children and friends. I wish I lived closer so we could have frequent visits. I enjoyed our long, leisurely mornings and evenings together. I want to contribute to your well-being.

You looked so beautiful and sporty in the new Eddie Bauer blouse and pants. You even wear casual clothes with a natural, elegant grace. I hope you enjoy them. And, since you like fresh flowers in the house, have them often. We all deserve a little beauty and luxury in our lives.

Another result of my visit home is a desire to write to you about an important issue that always seems just below the surface of our conversation, and one that is difficult for me to approach. We circled the subject the night we had dinner with the Lemasters and the Taylors, and R.C. was "fishing" for information about my personal life. Then, the next day, you encouraged me to see the movie *Sleepless in Seattle,* and I felt after seeing it, that perhaps in your loving way, you were worried about my romantic happiness. In my heart I feel you already instinctively know—that I am gay. I am homosexual. For the first time in my life, I feel the need to share this with you—not out of a selfish desire, but in some gentle way and from a loving need to put your mind at ease—to assure you that I am not alone.

Allen and I have had a long-term committed relationship for almost fourteen years. He is my mate. And like any long-term relationship, it has its ups and downs. But we share a generous, loving, supportive companionship that fosters our mutual well-being. Whatever your feelings about homosexuality, either from a religious view or from the standpoint of the wise and loving mother you have always been, I know this news may be troubling and confusing; but also, I hope, a relief. I know some things, Mother, and I believe some things. I know God is love. I believe God loves us all and wants us to strive for love above all else. My love for Allen is a journey along that path. And in these troubled times of AIDS, we are healthy, monogamous, and safe.

Allen and I are known and respected in the

local community as a couple, and we are wel-
comed into the homes of many loving friends.
The board and staff of both the factory and restaurant know we are a couple, and we are generously
accepted as such.

I have hesitated for so long to tell you, fearing
that you might pull away from me, or in some
way feel responsible for my sexual orientation, as
parents often do. You are NOT responsible. This
orientation is not a learned behavior or matter of
choice. It just is. It is as much a part of my identity
as blond hair and green eyes. Something deep in
my being knows that. I finally acknowledged and
accepted the fact when I was a freshman in college. I am as reasonably happy and as well adjusted
in this crazy world as the next person and am
grateful to get the chance to "make one someone
happy" as Jimmy Durante so delightfully sings in
the *Sleepless in Seattle* score. Love IS the answer.
The fundamental things DO apply . . . as time
goes by.

I decided to write to you about this important
part of my life rather than bring it up in casual
conversation, because I know the news may take
a while to digest. I finally realized I was unhappy
with the situation, that my friends and coworkers
knew me better than my own family did.

Perhaps I have underestimated your ability to
understand by not sharing this news before now,

and I ask for your forgiveness if that is the case. I guess we both felt uncomfortable approaching the subject. I leave it to you to decide whether or not you want to share this letter and this news with anyone else. I am comfortable with everyone knowing. The truth sets us free. It's 1993. I'm forty-three years old. We're adults, grown up, and able to see through the fog of prejudice.

I stand before you with my heart revealed, with my arms tightly around you, with as loving an embrace as ever a son could give.

May the Lord keep us and bless us.

I love you,

Jeff

CHAPTER NINETEEN

Becoming Better People

One day, I went on the air and asked anyone listening who had been served by a particular nonprofit organization to tell a story about how it helped improve the quality of their lives. We were impressed by what we heard. Besides making me feel better about paying my taxes, these stories were proof that, despite all the terrible things that go on, it's still a loving world.

HEAVEN ON EARTH

I was intrigued when I first heard about Camp Hemlocks, run by Easter Seals in Hebron, Connecticut. Camp Hemlocks is 160 acres of trails, swimming ponds, crafts buildings, dining halls, horseback riding rings, archery areas, every square inch of it designed for people with a multitude of disabilities. I kept wondering what it must feel like to disabled people to find one place, finally, so welcoming, and where so many things are possible.

I began by reading a short poem about Camp Hemlocks, written by Susan Schwartz, who has multiple sclerosis.

Diagnosed and full of fear
that I'd be left behind,
Unaware of the myriad ways that
people could be kind,
I never dreamed that I would find
A world designed with me in mind.
Closed out,
I thought, from restaurants where
I had wined and dined,
by entrances with steps instead of ramps
that are inclined, and many
other obstacles that just serve to remind
me that my world is so imperfectly
designed.
It so often seemed to me
that architects were blind,
and the surfaces I rode on seemed
to have been mined,
and more and more it seemed to me my life
could be defined as
begrudgingly routine. Just
a daily grind.

But for the last three years,
Camp Hemlocks has been my

vacation find.
Here you come from around
the world, so eager
to be kind.
And for ten days
I get to leave the other world behind,
and share with you this happy world
that you designed with me
in mind.

Susan joined us by telephone from her New York City home. "I am more free at Camp Hemlocks than anywhere else in my life because of being able to move around from place to place. I'm in a sip-and-puff wheelchair that I drive with my mouth. I puff to go forward and sip to go back. I use a softer puff or sip to go left and right. It's a little confusing in the beginning but after a couple of months one masters it. At the camp, there are no barriers and the scenery is fabulous. To be able to move freely through the buildings and nature paths is a wonderful liberty for me. And there are activities I can do there that I cannot do normally, like poetry and learning to paint using a brush in my mouth."

To paint, a long, lightweight stick brush is inserted in Susan's mouth and the watercolors are taped to the easel. She said, "The paintings I've made with my mouth are prettier than anything I had ever done with my hands."

As our phone lines filled up, Cathy Usher joined me

in the studio to tell about some of her experiences at the camp. Here is our conversation.

CATHY: About eight years ago we were what you'd call a normal, happy family. My husband and I were both working. We had two children. Everybody said, "Wow, you're like the perfect family."

FAITH: And then something more challenging came along?

CATHY: Then my daughter fell off a seesaw the third week into kindergarten, and suffered a grand mal seizure; her whole right side was involved. Prior to her injury, Beth was on the soccer and swim teams and took dancing lessons. Afterward, she was left with little use of her right side; she had lost her right visual field in both eyes and had speech difficulty.

FAITH: You had no idea that a place like Camp Hemlocks existed?

CATHY: And when I found out, in my ignorance, I said, "I am not sending my child to a camp for disabled children! She's going to fit into a regular camp." Well, I looked for that perfect camp and couldn't find it. Begrudgingly, I went to Camp Hemlocks.

FAITH: How did Beth respond at first?

CATHY: When she got there and saw that there were people just like her, she let down her guard. Right away, a child came running over to her and said, "Hi, Beth, I'm Dawn and I'm going to be your buddy." And off they went. I was choking back tears as I walked away. I sat by the phone the entire time. When I went to pick her up,

I'm telling you, I saw a different child. She was smiling and laughing. She said, "Mommy, I played floor hockey and basketball! I went boating, swimming, and fishing!" It was incredible to see this in a child who had gone through two years of agonizing physical therapy, when all she wanted and couldn't find anywhere was some enjoyment.

🌿

A caller, Leo, said it seems as if he has been at Camp Hemlocks forever. "I was leery at first but in my junior year of high school I tried out a summer session and it was the best vacation of my life. My disability is something called arthrogryposis multiplex congenita; I have limited use of my arms and upper body; I do most things I need to do with my feet. Camp Hemlocks was amazing because it opened my eyes to a barrier-free life. I had never done anything like horseback riding, but I did it there. And I did archery. That was seventeen years ago and I've been hooked ever since."

When I asked Leo about being with people who are like him, he said, "Sometimes it's a stressful situation for me to be out in public and do the things that other people take for granted. At Camp Hemlocks I don't feel like an outsider."

Alice's husband, Dan, underwent unexpected heart surgery at age sixty-nine, suffered a stroke, and was not expected to live. Alice said, "This was a tremendous shock to Dan and our family. He was a very active man;

it was difficult for him to accept what happened. He now has impaired vision, left-side paralysis, and has difficulty walking. I was nervous about the camp because Dan needed so much supervision, but he did go and enjoyed seeing other people with disabilities. I remember the first time he came home, he couldn't believe how a woman, an amputee, would swim in the pool and just enjoy herself. Dan makes things in arts and crafts and brings each one back for his granddaughter. She loves them."

Another caller, Ann, has been going to Hemlocks for twenty-five years. "I'd like to read you a story I wrote when I was in high school and I was being very sentimental about my life. It's called 'The Circle of Hemlock Trees.'

" 'Once upon a time, there was a little girl who, though she was different on the outside, was still the same on the inside. But because she was so different on the outside she seldom ventured from her home. She spent a great deal of time on her front porch watching the other children in her neighborhood play and wishing she could join them in their games. She was so sure that none of the other children would want to play with her that she never even tried.

" 'One day, when she was feeling especially lonely, a beautiful lady came strolling along and invited her to go for a walk. Normally, the little girl was too shy even to speak to strangers, but there was something so sweet and loving about the lady, and she decided to go along with her. As they walked, the little girl found that she did not tire as easily as she usually did. They climbed a mountain path, waded into a small stream, and crossed a large field where they came to a circle of hemlock trees. Inside the circle of trees, the little girl saw many other children who, like herself, were different on the outside but very much the same on the inside. They were all singing a song about joy and love and peace, and even though the little girl had never heard the song before, she began to sing.

" 'The little girl stayed with her new friends in the circle of the hemlock trees for a while, but soon it was time for her to return home, back across the field, through the stream and down the mountain path. Every once in a while, the little girl goes back to visit her dear friends in the circle of the hemlock trees, but most of the time she is too busy playing with the children in her neighborhood.' "

I asked Ann about her disability. "I have a disease so rare that no one has ever heard of it. Basically, I'm a little person, three feet two inches tall. As a child I had to wear a variety of braces so I felt different, you know? People were always staring at me like a freak and asking me questions I couldn't answer. Then I went to Camp Hemlocks and I was like any other kid. In my teen years I could have independence there from my family. I met my husband at the camp when I was twenty. We've been married six years. I'm thirty-three."

When Ann hung up, I watched Cathy's face change to delight as she listened in the studio. She told our listeners that she, too, has grown from her experiences at Camp

Hemlocks. "I remember when my able-bodied son volunteered there to be a 'buddy' to another child. He was nervous about going and when I said to be careful because they would match him with a disabled child, he said, annoyed, 'Okay, okay!' At the end of the weekend, I couldn't believe it. He came running in the door and said, 'Mom! Benny and I did a ropes course. We went swimming. We played field hockey.' And, in my ignorance, I said, 'I thought you were going to be paired up with a disabled boy.' And my son looked up at me, he was only ten at the time, and said, 'Well, he's in a wheelchair, does that mean he has a disability?' It hit me that we've got to stop seeing people as what they have. At Hemlocks, my son saw people in wheelchairs, people with missing limbs, but they were kids just like him."

This year, Cathy's son was matched with a nine year old named Mike. At one point, Mike said he had always wanted to feel a bat connect with a baseball. The next afternoon, Cathy's son picked up Mike's hands, wrapped them around a bat, and when the pitch came, they hit the ball.

ORGAN DONORS

*F*riend and volunteer associate producer Libby Patton walked into my office and said, "I think you should do a show about people on waiting lists for organ transplants." Libby knew an elderly woman who would become blind without a transplant, and I knew a young man, a father, who would have died without a new heart. I asked each of these people to tell their stories on the air, and I opened the phones for a kind of town meeting on our unspoken anxieties about donating organs.

I began by saying, "There are certain life-altering experiences that change you whether you're ready for them or not. You reconsider your priorities. You think about what in your life has meaning. You focus on your most important relationships.

"The premier life-altering experience is coming face-to-face with your own death, which you learn will come in a predetermined time. Today's show is about life-altering moments as seen through the eyes of those who need organ transplants.

"Please don't shut off the radio. The subject of donating organs might scare us because we have to think about how vulnerable we are. Please understand that in this show I hope to give something to you, not take something from you.

"You're about to meet a man who is alive because he has a new heart. You'll also meet a woman who has been waiting by the phone, afraid to leave the house, because she might miss the call from the organ donor staff saying a cornea has become available. These two people who share a great deal have never met each other. They will meet on our show. Many of us do not realize how important organ donations and tissue transplants are, or what it's like to receive one."

Then I looked up into the face of William Hurt look-alike Gar Rowbotham, now forty-three years old, and I asked him how long his new heart had been beating in his body.

GAR: Since that miraculous day, five years and two months ago.

FAITH: Explain how serious heart problems were in your family.

GAR: It took the lives of my mother, brother, two sisters, and my uncle, all by the age of forty. I had to watch from the sidelines and wonder if I was next.

Gar's heart did begin to fail, and by 1988, just after the birth of his son, he wrote in his diary, "I can't breathe at all, can't sleep unless propped up on a pillow, and only then for a few hours at a time. It's getting harder and harder to do anything physical. My hands and feet are frozen from poor circulation. I take several baths every day in an attempt to keep warm. I can't make it upstairs without great difficulty, and I sleep downstairs. It's Christmas, as we decorate our tree I realize this may be my last, and I cry with my son Sammy. I haven't lived enough. I am terrified of abandoning my boys, Bobbie [his wife], and my life."

While Gar was on the waiting list for a new heart, he battled depression and complete loss of hope. Friendship saved him. "Two weeks before a transplant I was at a real low," he said. "I lost my commitment to life. One of my friends more or less kicked me in the rear and got me really angry by telling me I had lost my commitment. It was like telling me I was worthless. It got me really mad and it got me in touch with the fact that I really wanted to live."

A new heart became available just in time to save Gar's life. He was told only that the heart was from a Caucasian male of his age who had lived and died in Manchester, New Hampshire. After delivering this brief description, the hospital transplant team quickly left Gar's room and sped off by helicopter, cooler in hand, to retrieve the heart.

The recipients of organs from other people adjust psychologically in many different ways. Some claim they crave different foods, only to learn that these foods were a favorite of the donor. Rowbotham frowns at such speculation, though I was to learn later that he was more confused by the experience than he let on during the show.

"You need a lot of help and understanding to figure out what's really going on," Gar explained. "After a transplant you go through this incredible sensorial transformation; all your senses become greater. It's easy to ascribe your feelings to the transplanted organ. The problem is that if you're really going to integrate your body and your spirit, this doesn't empower you or help you heal in a complete way. You really have to try to understand that all that you feel is coming from within you."

When the transplant team was ready with the new heart and Gar was prepared to undergo anesthesia, he did not know whether he would ever see his family and friends again. When he did survive the surgery, and for several weeks after, he was euphoric. And then mood swings began to set in. This is the point when some patients succeed and others do not. "You have to get through this rejection period," Gar said. "You have to cope with ingesting thousands of milligrams of liquid steroids in a relatively short period of time. No matter what the doctors and nurses tell you, there's no way they can prepare you for what this can do. You can feel your body going somewhere else and you don't know what to do. At one point I just couldn't function. I had three nurses bathing me. I didn't care, I was helpless."

To cope with the changes he was facing, including a long recuperation period, Gar says he decided to approach it as an executive would. He assembled a team of experts from different fields for mental and physical support. He attended sessions of the Exceptional Cancer Patients organization at Yale New Haven Hospital.

Gar told our listeners that his spiritual transformation was the most significant change he underwent. "When you go down that deep and come back up," Gar said, "you find out who you are. It starts with the question, do you choose life? We go through life never being faced with that question. I say that one does not begin to live until one is faced with it and chooses consciously."

I asked Gar if the next question he faced was, why am I here? "I've thought about it quite a bit," he said. "It's pretty simple. I think we're here to help each other through the struggle and to face ourselves. I think the most difficult and courageous thing that any individual has to do in life is to come to terms with yourself and your purpose; it's different for each of us. You don't have to have a near-death experience to face that. Unfortunately, sometimes we have to get to a difficult point to take an honest look at ourselves."

When I wondered about the world seeing him as the walking transplant thing, because of his public appearances, he explained, "I want to give people a sense that life is special for them. When I tell them what I've been through, it shocks them because I'm young, I look good. Because of my presence, they have to start looking at themselves and at life. In a sense I represent real hope and real possibility."

About signing a card signifying ourselves as organ donors, Gar said to our listeners, "My God, I don't think I consciously checked the donor card thinking I would need it. Now it is clear to me how empowering it is to check off that box."

❦

The other transplant recipient who inspired our show is seventy-eight-year-old Marian Miller. Marian was rapidly losing sight in one eye, and waiting anxiously, day after day, hoping the phone would ring with the news that a cornea had become available in time. Because many transplant centers will only call back the potential recipient for two hours before moving on to the next name on the waiting list, Mrs. Miller was afraid to leave her home for dinner, groceries, appointments, the normal business of life.

Each ring of the telephone brings hope and, to some degree, disappointment, for those who wait. "You have to believe in fate," Mrs. Miller told our listeners. She said her husband also helped her with his constant faith. "He would say to me he was sure I was going to get it, and I would say, 'I hope you're right.' I was quite blue."

Miraculously, as Mrs. Miller was preparing herself for our live telephone interview, the phone rang and it was the donor center informing her that a cornea had become available. She told the world about her news, just a few minutes old, live on our show. We wanted to give her a chance to speak with family and friends who would be thrilled to hear her news, and so we asked her to do only one other thing. I invited her to speak with Gar, sitting next to me in the studio, about their common experience.

GAR: Hello, Mrs. Miller.

MRS. MILLER: Hello, Gar.

GAR: What struck me is that you said you were really blue two weeks ago. I was at the bottom of a barrel two weeks before my transplant, so I found a real parallel with you. You sound like such a sweet person. You sound literally, and figuratively, like a good-hearted person. It sounds like your faith is strong. I feel great for you.

MRS. MILLER: Well, thank you very much. Of course, I don't compare my situation to yours at all because lots of people can lose vision in one eye but you have the other one. It wasn't life-threatening like yours was.

GAR: It's still scary, though.

MRS. MILLER: Oh, yes.

FAITH: You both must feel so much for those who are still waiting for the phone to ring.

MRS. MILLER: Especially young people. I'm older, I'm seventy-eight. A young person would have a much harder time, I think.

GAR: I think it's great that you had the courage to attempt this at seventy-eight. You're making a very positive statement to people your age.

MRS. MILLER: Thank you so much. I think your story is just wonderful.

At the time of our show, the official waiting list for organs and tissues was forty-five hundred people in New England alone. I realized for the first time that in an instant I could be someone in need of a donor.

I heard from many concerned listeners when we opened the phones to them, including Ellen. "I am very interested to hear from Mrs. Miller because in the early 1960s, our family filled out donor cards and had my mother do it, too. When she died in our hospital, they took her corneas for transplant. I got a letter from the Eye Bank about three weeks later saying how happy the recipients were. It was one of the few things that helped me with my grief, to think that somebody was going to be looking out of Mom's eyes."

❧

What my listeners that afternoon did not know, and I felt he deserved time to digest it, was that on that very morning, Gar Rowbotham awoke with one thing on his mind—finding out who his donor was. While not every recipient needs to know, Gar saw it as "the last piece of the puzzle." He was up early and drove from Connecticut to New Hampshire and back in one day. The way Gar located the home of his donor is an interesting story.

He said that when the transplant team appeared by his bedside, they explained that they were taking off by helicopter to Manchester, New Hampshire, to pick up his new heart. Gar stored this information away. And when he was a little stronger, he called a close friend and asked him to drive to Manchester and search the obituaries in the town newspaper for the death of a man close to his age. There was a story about a man who had committed suicide.

On the morning Gar was to join me, he drove to Manchester and searched for the address mentioned in the obituary. He located it at a trailer in a small trailer park. Gar said he screwed up his courage and knocked on the door of another trailer close by. Luckily, the man who answered was friendly and a longtime resident. He told Gar that the man he was inquiring about had lost his job and become despondent. The neighbor said he still wonders if he could have helped the man in some way.

Gar said the conversation was over but he could not

leave without asking his most important question. "Was he a good person?"

The man said he was.

UNABLE TO READ OR WRITE

Producer Diane Orson and I received a letter from the state chapter of Literacy Volunteers, which matches volunteer tutors with clients who may not be able to read, write, or, in the case of immigrants, even understand English. We agreed to ask for stories from listeners who have been involved in literacy.

It was Valentine's Day when we did the show. I began, "If love is caring deeply about what happens to another person, and I think that's a pretty good definition, then the people I'm interested in hearing from today show love to complete strangers. They volunteer to teach reading and writing to adults who can do neither. What happens to the volunteer teacher and to that adult student when a real connection is made? Literacy Volunteers of America, based here in Connecticut, knows what an important working relationship this can be. They estimate, and I was amazed at this number, that three hundred thousand adults in Connecticut alone are functionally illiterate, and they often live their lives 'passing,' with the secret that they cannot read or write. Today I would like to hear from literacy volunteers or adult clients.

"I've been given permission to read a short essay entered in a Literacy Volunteers of America contest. It was written by a Connecticut man, Donald Denham. When he began working with Literacy Volunteers, he could not read or write. After years of hard work with volunteer Beth GrosJean, he was able to write what I will now read in Mr. Denham's handwriting, just as he wrote it:

" 'I read a book, it was called *The Black Stallion*. I know it don't mean much to most people but it meant a lot to me. You see one year and a half-ago I could not read a Book. It don't seem like a big deal unless you spent your life unable to read. I guess some people take reading like it was nothing but I know different. To read a book like *The Black Stallion* is invigorating like I have never felt before. It was like I was there and when I came to the end I cried. For 46 years I never Knew it could be like this. I don't know if this is the type of letter you are looking for but I believe that I have won already because I could write this to you about the book I read.' "

We received lots of calls from all kinds of people who were giving time as literacy volunteers, and we heard from adult learners who were American and foreign-born. Sheila is African American, though most people who are illiterate are white.

SHEILA: My biggest goal was to get my high school diploma. I am in my thirties and I just never thought I could do it. I heard about Literacy Volunteers, so I called them one day and that was it. They connected me with the best tutor I could ever have had.

FAITH: What made you take action?

SHEILA: I would get totally frustrated trying to help

my four kids with their homework, and they would get frustrated because I couldn't. It's hard to tell your fourth grader you don't comprehend what you read. All my life reading was a goal I wanted to achieve. I quit school when I was in the seventh grade. I'm from down south.

FAITH: Why did you quit?

SHEILA: I felt like I was a failure. I didn't like school. The teachers were very . . . I don't know, it was so different then. You had to read aloud in front of the class and I had a very bad complex about that. It was just something I couldn't do. They would actually fail me because I could not read in front of the class.

FAITH: Do you want to name the Literacy Volunteers tutor who worked with you?

SHEILA: Mildred O'Brien. She was like a mother to me all the way through. Any time I would get discouraged, she would lift my spirits right back up. She was very persuasive. She just said, "You can do it!"

FAITH: How did it turn out?

SHEILA: I got my high school diploma last year and we had a big celebration. We hired a band and rented a hall.

FAITH: And what did you feel that night?

SHEILA: I felt like a queen.

❧

One night, I was invited to a meeting of Literacy Volunteers in the Westbrook, Connecticut, library. The room was crowded with men and women of different ages and circumstances. The service they offer costs nothing and gives so much. I wondered how many more citizen volunteers were gathered across the country with a common purpose, to give another human being the freedom that literacy provides.

CHAPTER TWENTY

Bruce: A Continuing Partnership

If I had six months left on earth, I would spend considerable time with Bruce Clements. He is one of the dearest people in my life, someone who has made me feel the most myself. No matter what we are doing or saying, I have a sense of luxury from knowing in the deepest way that the time we spend together simply matters.

Our friendship began twenty-five years ago in college, where Bruce was my English professor, and now we collaborate every month on the air. For several years, Bruce has joined me in exploring many of the unusual themes that are discussed on my show—the value of having a dual life, the moment you realized life was more complicated than you thought, when you shocked yourself by something you said or did.

Bruce and I were sitting at a small table in one of our favorite hangouts, a New Haven café called Koffee, where I began trying to reconstruct our history together for this book. I was midway through a complicated scenario, when Bruce leaned over and said in that direct, elegant way he has, "I have known you for all of your adult life!" I laughed, and as he went on talking, I found myself looking at his face, thinking that it is as if I have always known him. I wonder how I could ever explain the size of his heart or the depth of his honesty and intelligence. It is best described, perhaps, in the love and devotion Bruce feels for a truly lovely woman, his wife, Hanna. He told me once how much he enjoys accompanying her to events so that he can watch her at work in the room. Or how happy he is to have an answering machine because he can hear Hanna's voice. One day, Bruce brought along a sheet of paper and read me the poems he had written to Hanna in honor of her birthday, and how he had cried reading them in front of their adult children, and when I heard them, I cried, too. Bruce sees what is really there.

He spends his days trying to be part of what is good in the world. For Bruce, as for many of us, generosity is as natural as breathing.

Now he appears once a month at my studio door and I madly type out a few lines of explanation to open the show, while Bruce does what he always does five minutes before we go on the air—he takes off his shoes and socks, empties his pockets of keys and change, and grabs a yellow legal pad for doodles and notes. While the show theme comes up and fills our headphones, I have to admit that I sometimes sit there anxious, wondering if this will be the day that no one calls. Somehow they always do.

Bruce once suggested that we ask for stories attached to an article of clothing. My own attic is filled with clothes that represent my life decade by decade. One important story came from a caller who described an incident to us that occurred soon after her mother's death. The night of the wake she stood in her mother's room, looking into her box of jewelry on the dresser. "I said to myself, I guess this is mine now," and we could hear in her voice how odd and moving the moment was. She carefully chose to wear a pair of her mother's earrings to the wake that evening. After the service, someone in attendance had brought along photographs of her mother, including one of her mother at our caller's christening. The picture showed her mother holding her in her arms. "And there in the picture my mother was wearing the very same earrings I had chosen for her wake."

ADMITTING YOU WERE WRONG

As Bruce pointed out during one of our shows, some politicians have perfected the "no-fault confession," in which they try to look good by saying, "Mistakes were made." So we did a show on the value of admitting when we were wrong. One of our favorite callers, Tess, learned a lesson about apologies from her father. "Whenever I would finally admit I was wrong, and sometimes it would take a while, he would tell me to go to my room and think about it; that's all he would say. I would go up there and stew and hum and worry; finally, he'd come up there and say that the best thing about the whole situation was that I'd been honest and he admired me for it. But, then, in grade school, I was baffled. A little boy had done something in class, and the teacher began ranting and raving, demanding to know who'd done it. The boy said he had, and the teacher praised him, saying, 'You're a great George Washington for admitting it.' She told our whole class to look up to him as somebody of honor. A couple of days later, something of a similar nature happened, and when a little black girl confessed, the teacher stood there dead silent, looking at her, and then she lit into this child like there was no tomorrow. She said she was an awful little girl who didn't belong in our class, and that we should all stay away from her for the rest of the day. I was mortified sitting there. The first thing I did when I got home was talk to my dad, and I learned an important lesson. He listened to my story and said, 'Sometimes you have to size up who you're going to be honest to.' "

THE MEANING OF CLASS

*B*ruce came up with the idea to try a call-in show asking for stories about people who have demonstrated that they have real class. Along with Bruce, who is one of the classiest people I have ever met, I thought of our radio psychologist, Dr. Nancy Horn, in New Haven. When I asked her on the air what she feels her purpose is, she said, "To give value to people and things." She's classy, too.

Among the callers who phoned us that day was Eileen, who nominated her daughter. "Last week, my family stopped in Baltimore during our vacation, and as we sat at a beautiful spot overlooking the harbor, we saw a man in raggy clothes begging for money. Hundreds of people were passing him by, not giving him anything. He said he was thirsty and wanted to buy lemonade. We didn't stop for him, either. My daughter, Sarah, turned around and asked, 'Why don't we give him some money?' and I began this lecture about how we don't know if he really needs it to buy beer and drugs. And my daughter looked at me and said, 'Of course he needs it, look at him.' I felt so ashamed; she was right, and she was the only one in the crowd who gave him money. At age twelve she had more class than any of us, and we not only learned a lesson from her, we realized she was the person we had hoped she'd become."

A CLASSY CITY

*E*laine told a story about her son, who had just driven home from the other side of the country. "It was one of those very rainy nights, and at midnight he reached the George Washington Bridge in New York. He'd been on a tight budget; he realized he was penniless, and the people at the toll booth told him to pull over. He was sitting there thinking that he was in big trouble when all of a sudden a stranger knocked on his window, threw his arms out to him, and said, 'Welcome to New York!' Then he handed him five dollars. The bridge toll was four dollars and after that there was one more toll of a dollar. I told my son he'd met his guardian angel."

❧

Cathy phoned to defend an uncle she says many people think of as weird. "I converted two years ago from the family's religion to another religion, and several of my relatives, including my parents, got horribly upset about it. Every time I see them, they're constantly asking, 'Why did you reject your religion?' One day, after sitting there listening to me defend myself, my uncle jumped in and said, 'You know, she has a very strong faith. She believes in God. She made her choice and I respect her for that.' And he was the same religion as my family, too. I felt that was really classy. Another time, he was very, very ill in the hospital. My sister and brother and I went into New York to see him and we were uncomfortable. He was emaciated and looked terrible because he was in pain, and each of us had to go in separately. He led the conversation, asking us questions about what we were doing, and he made each of us comfortable. When my sister and brother and I talked afterward, we realized that he had talked about totally different things with each of us, yet we all felt the same way."

KEEPING SECRETS FROM CLOSE FRIENDS

I once kept a secret from people close to me because knowing the secret would have put them in jeopardy. It was perhaps the heaviest burden I have endured. Bruce told the listeners that children can keep secrets so that someone will ask them what's wrong. "When I was in high school, I stayed out of school for three straight weeks; I just didn't go. My mother was disturbed when she found out, and went to see our family physician about it. And he said, 'Well, thank God, because he was due to rebel.' The important thing is that my mother came home and told me every word he said. They were both first-rate human beings."

I learned when we did a show on this subject that some people are just as glad not to know our secrets. Gil, Christian youth director of a church, explained the dilemma. "I was given a secret to hold when a fifteen-year-old girl told me that she and her boyfriend had become sexually active. She said she wanted to go on birth control and wanted my opinion, which I gave her. The problem is that her parents are my best friends, and, of course, I know they would want to know anything that would affect their daughter, as I would about my own daughter. But telling them would violate the daughter's trust in me. My head has been spinning over this. I told our pastor and she agreed that there is no way that I could violate the confidence of the girl; it would ruin my credibility with all the other children. If I had it to do again, I would have said when she explained the subject, 'Let me put you in touch with someone you can talk to.' " Gil said it felt good just to tell someone. I appreciated how carefully he was trying to sort out his loyalties and responsibilities.

WHEN LIFE IS MORE COMPLICATED THAN YOU IMAGINED

In keeping confidences we discover that comprehending complexity is a lifelong process. Bruce and I asked for stories that show this, and Elizabeth got us rolling with her memory of making her First Holy Communion. "In those days there were rails on the altar and the priest stood behind them. My mother explained to me that God loves everyone, and I said to her, 'Then how come only boys can be on the altar?' I remember that she was unable to answer me. That has stuck with me my whole life; there have been many railings and altars since then."

Then Susan phoned us, saying she grew up with nine brothers and sisters in New Haven. "I realized things were complicated when I was in high school. It was 1972 and I was going to graduate in three years instead of four. They told me that I had to graduate second in my class, not first, because it was not appropriate for a girl to graduate first. So this boy who was number two graduated first. At the time, it was, well, I guess this is the way it is, a man's world. But twenty-two years later I still think, 'Oh, my God.' I have four kids now and I've been working on college part-time for many years. I've finally graduated. Thank God I don't have any daughters because I would be in such pain for them. Women have come a long way but they haven't come very far."

When Doug called to explain his story about complications, Bruce and I couldn't help laughing. "It happened when I heard from an old college friend; he had just gotten married and we agreed to get together with our wives downtown. We walked in and both my wife and I gasped, because my wife had been going out with my buddy for four years prior to my knowing about it, and I had been going out with my buddy's wife for four years prior to his knowing about it." At first I told Doug I was sure he was making this up, but he was so sincere in his telling of it that I ended up believing him. He said the two women became instant best friends. Apparently his own wife broke the ice by saying, "This could only happen in a Danielle Steel novel."

There is one more caller I admired for the way she faced a complicated situation. Christien told us she had just graduated from high school in Georgia. "I believe that I was the only person in my school who had the views I have now. The town that I'm from is right in the middle of the Bible Belt; we were an entirely white county. I was raised that it doesn't matter what color they are, and who cares about their sexual preference? One day, sitting in class, we were having a pro-life, pro-choice

debate, and I'm the only one in there who was pro-
choice and I just wanted to be heard. I had boys, juniors
in high school and they're pretty big, in my face telling
me how wrong I am even to think that way, and that I'm
a murderer. They were very, very crude, and I was
shocked and scared. I was hearing this from my generation, which is supposed to be so understanding and live
for now. These were my friends, people I had grown up
with. I would speak to my girlfriends about it and they
would always say, 'Oh, yeah, if I ever did, then I would.'
I also know that if some of the guys in the class got their
girlfriends pregnant, I think that would have been the
choice they made. Teen pregnancy was a problem at our
school. It was the hypocrisy of the situation. I'm ashamed
to say that I lost it and I started to cry and scream. I think
the whole experience awakened me to trying to find out
what other people think, to become more rounded. I
don't want to put anybody in the situation I was in; I still
have nightmares about it."

WHEN DID YOU SHOCK YOURSELF?

*I*t was a conversation his friend had at Christmas that
prompted Bruce's idea to ask listeners about a time when
they said or did something that shocked them. We went
on the air and Bruce began with a story. "There was a
man during the Vietnam War who had determined that
he was going to Canada, but he had not told his parents,

who were very patriotic in the traditional sense. It was Christmas dinner, and his aunt was there, who said to him, 'What are you going to do in the coming year?' And all of a sudden he said, 'I'm leaving the country, I'm going to Ottawa, Canada. . . .' Then he gave the date, and talked about the war. His parents had no idea; the presence of a third person enabled him to do it. Others have said to me that when something like that happens, it's as if you're a spectator at your own amazing performance."

When we opened the phone lines, there were several memorable stories, starting with Dan's about the day he came upon a highway car accident. "The driver, a young girl, was hysterical, and the car was totaled. I got inside the car with her and tried to calm her down until the police and the fire department got there. I don't know why I did it, I just did. Another time, in a similar situation, I did exactly the opposite, and shocked myself. A convertible was turned over on the highway, and an off-duty state trooper says to me, 'Let's turn this car over.' I just said, 'No.' I don't know why. Was it that I didn't know what to expect underneath? Did I not want to touch anybody who was hurt until the police came? It was a complete shock to me."

Bruce's friend Helga McKinley, a psychotherapist in Albany, New York, joined us on the show and told a story of her own. "My story starts way back when I was a little girl in Vienna, Austria. In 1938, the country was taken over by Hitler, and many bad things happened to my family; my life changed drastically. When I came to this country, I learned English, and I chose never to discuss what happened; it was very painful. Fifty years passed. Then, on the fiftieth anniversary of November tenth, which is called *Kristallnacht* in Europe, representing the time when Germans smashed the windows of thousands of synagogues and shops, there were many memorial services throughout the country. A young little rabbi who played the guitar and looked about twelve years old happened to meet me somewhere, and he asked if I would tell what I experienced. I had never thought of sharing this with anyone, but I said, 'Yes,' to my great surprise. I went to the synagogue to tell his small congregation about my story, and during the question-and-answer period afterward, someone said to me, 'You seem to have lived a kind of normal life even though you experienced an awful lot as a young person. How were you able to live a normal life?' And I answered, to my great surprise, 'It's because of him,' pointing to my husband, who sat in the last row. I didn't even know I thought that. It was very nice. And since that night my husband and I never discussed it; I think we were both embarrassed."

❧

A listener named Betsy remembered her first day of college many years ago. "I had been on the campus for

about a half hour, when I decided to leave my dorm
room and visit a friend who was moving in as a freshman
in her dorm. On the way, I ran into a handsome young
man, and because we had mutual friends, I spent some
time with him that afternoon. He came to my dorm
room, where we met my new roommate for the first
time, and when he left, she asked, 'Who was that? Was
that your boyfriend?' And with no forethought, I said,
'No, his name is Al Something, but I'm going to marry
him someday.' And I was as shocked as she was that I said
it. There was this knowing there. Last April, Al and I
celebrated our silver anniversary. For thirty-one years,
through ups and downs, that serenity of just knowing has
always been there."

Our final caller that afternoon told a story I will remember for a long time. Hugh's story was about a friend
of his mother's. "It was the 1950s, back in the days of no
copy machines, and this gentleman had just completed
the finished draft of his doctoral dissertation in France.
He took his two handwritten copies to the bindery to
have them bound. As he was bringing them back, he was
crossing the river on a bridge, and he suddenly had an
impulse to throw his work of many years in the water.
He threw his dissertation away and never became a professor. He's still quite an expert in his field." Hugh went
on to say that the story was relevant to him because he is
writing his own dissertation, and he added, "I also think
there's something universal about this impulse to jump off

bridges. The gentleman strikes me as a heroic figure in a very sad sense. It doesn't seem pathological; somehow I think what he did was liberating."

We ended the show with one last exchange between Hugh and Bruce:

BRUCE: Are you writing your dissertation on a word processor?

HUGH: Yes.

BRUCE: Do you push the save button often?

HUGH: Yes.

BRUCE: Good! One hero of that kind in any given century is exactly the right number.

SOME CATASTROPHES BRING GIFTS

Losing my parents when I was young is not an experience that I would wish on anyone, but I must admit that there were benefits that came out of those years. I became determined to make something of myself. I got to make more choices than many young adults do, about where to live, what to wear, who to have as friends, what to study in college. I also got to imagine what my parents might have wanted for me had they lived, and in this way I heard myself say what it was that I, not my parents, wished for. Perhaps best of all, I became especially close to my own siblings and their children.

This is why I was interested in Bruce's idea to ask listeners how catastrophes ended up giving them something in the end. Right away we assured callers that we knew some events do not result in anything good. For instance, Bruce said, "When I was twelve, a woman who had been taking care of my brother and me, and had said that she was going to leave someday and not come back, left and didn't come back. I think that was very hard on her. It was very hard on us. I think I did not learn anything from that. I felt dismayed and puzzled, and though now I understand a little better, I'm still sorry and I don't think I'm better because that happened."

Our first caller, Robin, said, "I was diagnosed with Hodgkin's lymphoma about four years ago. I'm doing extremely well, no recurrence. The brightest light has been my recent marriage and new life. I'm convinced that if it hadn't been for my illness, I wouldn't have met him. I was in a destructive relationship before I got sick. I went for counseling when I was diagnosed, and the counselor said, 'The most important thing you need to be doing now is taking care of yourself. Get rid of all the negative things in your life. Your relationship is a very negative thing.' He was right, and before long I got out. After that, believe it or not, I met my husband through a dating service. He's a wonderful man, and I have a different perspective on things I probably wouldn't have had."

When Claire reached us, she explained that it was eight years ago to the day that her mother died. "There were six children, and Mom was the one who managed everything. The children tended to support Mom more than Dad because their marriage wasn't very good. But with her death, which was devastating to all of us and her friends, we saw our father grow. He took on a lot of what Mom had done. It's too bad she never got to see him in this role because she would have been happy about it. It opened our eyes to what our father was all about, and that he loved us but couldn't show it. Every holiday now we get together, grandchildren and great-grandchildren, and we have more solidarity as a family."

A caller named Paulette learned something fifteen years ago that changed an important relationship. "I found out then that my brother was a heroin addict. He was stealing from his own family. Nobody could trust him. He was in and out of programs for help with his addiction. He did finally stop using because he was afraid he would get AIDS from sharing needles. He got his life back together, got a job, his own place, and eventually got back in touch with his ex-wife and children, and made peace with everyone. The sad part is that he did find out that he's HIV positive; he doesn't have full-blown AIDS. The irony is that the AIDS scare has given him years on his life that he would not have had. He's living for the first time in twenty years."

Maria spoke with a Spanish accent. I thought her story was remarkable. "About twenty-eight years ago, I had my fourth child, full-term, but he was to die soon after his birth. My mother and my husband—their personalities did not communicate. I had to be readmitted to the hospital, so the two of them had to bury the baby and take care of the three children at home. They became so close doing this together and they stayed that way from then on. Something bad brought them together. My mother died three years ago, but all those years there was something special that she had for him."

I was moved by what a caller named Hal had to say, because he noticed his father's vulnerability and never mistook it for weakness. "My grandfather was a very unpleasant man throughout his life, and he did not treat his family well. He was in business with his own son, my father, and that was not a good relationship. He was the kind of man who treated everyone dastardly for eleven months, until it was time for him to make it up to you with financial gifts at Christmas. When I was sixteen, my grandfather had to go into the hospital for a very difficult heart operation. After surgery, the hospital called my father with the news that he had passed away. My dad broke into tears and was greatly grief stricken. It made the rest of our family grieve, too, possibly for my father's feeling of pain. Seeing my father this way changed my life because it made me appreciate a different side of what love is. It expanded forever my understanding of how someone can be in your life, not as a beam of light or something wonderful, but still move you when you lose them."

The last caller, Sue, described how changed she was by an accident two decades ago. "I'm now forty, but when I was twenty, I was in a severe auto accident out in California; I was riding in a van-type vehicle when I was hit head-on; my legs were crushed, and I would have died if I hadn't been ten minutes from the UCLA Medical Center. Prior to the accident I was a music major, but during my hospitalization, with both legs in traction and my mouth wired shut for three months, I became interested in nursing. I had to learn to walk again at age twenty-one. It was difficult to become dependent at a time in your life when you're supposed to be branching out on your own. I've learned to have faith that things will come to you when you need them. I've just finished my master's at the Yale School of Nursing. I had an experience that changed my life in a second, and I'm really glad it did."

CHAPTER TWENTY-ONE

Counting Your Assets

When I was fourteen, my mother and I were spending the winter in West Palm Beach, Florida, because she was ill. On a late-afternoon walk, we came upon a food market on the edge of the black community and stopped by for a few things. I yanked a steel cart from the row and began wheeling it in the direction of the first aisle, when I accidentally struck a sixtyish black woman in the back of her ankles. I could see her surprise and the wince; naturally, I apologized. And then, just behind me, a white woman loudly said in a voice filled with venom, "Don't apologize to her!" We were all motionless for a long moment, and then, quietly, we returned to our tasks. Oddly, my mother and I barely spoke on the way home and we never again mentioned what happened. Nevertheless, I think of it as one of my wake-up calls. I can still summon the shock and sorrow I felt that things could be this way.

I decided to do a show on how being part of a minority community is an asset in one's life. What I remember most was how doing the show from a positive point of view seemed to amaze many listeners, especially those who live with prejudice daily.

A WHITE MAN UNDERSTANDS

Ray said, "I don't know what inspired you to have this topic but it's pretty neat. Adversity is a true test of character. In the early seventies I was trying to acquire an education at a time when the government felt it had wronged Hispanics, blacks, and Native Americans, and that it was right to make up for past errors. Unfortunately, I was one of the white people who had doors close on us because of affirmative action. The experience gave me insight. I can now appreciate the minority frustration, that for so long they had talents, skills, and gifts that were not cultivated. I had to believe in myself and I say to anyone who feels they don't have the opportunities they deserve, hang in there; have faith."

MORE SPIRITUAL

Like the previous caller, Carol is white, but she learned what racism is when she became a mother. "I have a son who is half black. I'm fourteen years into this and I have to say that his being half black has made me who I am. I've been alone with my son all along, and the gifts I've received from being his mother are immeasurable. The pain that I paid for it is probably also immeasurable, but I wouldn't trade any of it, especially learning how to persevere through all the trials and tribulations. You really do learn to identify with your strengths. I've become greatly in touch with my spirituality, and I've overcome many obstacles, including pursuing an education."

MAKE SOMETHING BETTER

Half Native American and half African American, Tom recalled his parents and their beliefs. "My parents always taught us that you have to work twice as hard to go half as far. Many people would see that as a negative thing to teach children but it helped us. My father always said, 'Chips are to be eaten, never to be worn. After a hard day's work, if you have surplus energy, fight to make something better.' I've been a teacher eighteen years. Although it is very painful at certain times to be a minority, when I'm in front of my kids I am upbeat and I believe in them more than they believe in themselves."

HAVING WHAT'S IMPORTANT

Tracy sounded amazed when she reached me. "This is incredible that the topic is the assets of being handicapped. I'm legally blind and that has provided quite a few assets, believe it or not. As a child, I was one of the first kids in my town to be mainstreamed and that wasn't an easy process; there were a lot of teachers who didn't want to change what they did so I could see it. It taught me at a young age to speak up about what my needs were. I had to because I didn't want to be different, I wanted to keep up with everyone else. I'm proud of a lot of things; I have a professional position in the community; I'm married to a wonderful man; and I just gave birth to a daughter. I have all the important things in life."

APPRECIATING OTHERS

*F*riends and family are what give Kay strength. "I think I'm more aware of the special qualities of people who are different because I'm an Asian American; my mother is Japanese and my father is Caucasian. I learned to rely on my family for emotional support but I also learned to appreciate my friends more because they were so supportive when they saw me struggling with prejudice."

THEY DON'T SPEAK FOR ME

*W*hen someone spray-painted slurs on the home of the mayor in West Hartford, Connecticut, I told our listeners there was something we could do. I began, "I'm at home here in my living room. Someone said once that wisdom is the ability to hold many things to be true at the same time. For instance, we are all the same and we are all different. And we have so much in common despite our differences. There are events which capitalize on our differences and cause us to ignore what is common to all of us. For example, when our economy is troubled and we have less money and security, I notice that we become angry and fearful, and we look for someone to blame. We aim our frustrations at those who are different, gays, blacks, Jews, Indians, etc. Incidents of discrimination rise when the economy falls.

"Along with events, there are people who ignore what is common in all of us. As children, these people are taught prejudice, and as adults, they continue to capitalize on our differences. Wisely, our country was founded on the principle that we must protect the minority, especially when they are least popular, lest they be trampled by the majority. This has helped us keep our balance as a nation. Still, there are days when the scales tip dangerously out of balance, like now, when our local economy is hurting.

"Within the past year we have seen a dramatic rise in hate crimes against people who are African American, gay and lesbian, against immigrants of all kinds, American Indians, the disabled, and, as always, against women. We have witnessed desecration of Jewish synagogues, and, most recently, a swastika and hateful words were spray-painted on the home of the West Hartford mayor, who is Jewish.

"What we can do is refuse to be silent about it. I invite you to send a message that those who act on hate or prejudice do not speak for you."

Robert Leikind, head of the Connecticut chapter of

the Anti-Defamation League, joined me on the show, and, happily, our phones rang and rang.

UNDERSTANDING AND APPRECIATION

BERNADETTE: I am happy to say here that I have been very upset that others are being hurt, criticized, and put down, just for being who they are. No one has been able to convince me to hate a certain race because of past events. My father is a bitter Native American who is totally against Jews and blacks. Being of the lower part of society and having to live in places that have poverty, I have come to realize that we are all one people, that we all have hearts. We cannot take things out on one another because of what other generations have done. The Bible talks about how God made all the generations and all generations are to be with Him.

FAITH: You mentioned that your father does not like African Americans. Has he been able to accept your child?

BERNADETTE: His first comment was, "Get rid of the black child; otherwise, you'll ruin your life." He didn't say it this pleasantly. I refused to listen to it. It's been nineteen months and he has shown a little bit of consideration. He has glanced at her and given her Christmas gifts, but he still talks negatively about the black community as a whole. I have tried to show him that in every race mistakes have been made. I learned about the Holocaust and the suffering they have had to go through; every aspect of their lives was full of pain. And I see African Americans the same way.

STAND TOGETHER

EDGAR: I've always been frightened of anti-Semitism; I'm Jewish and I have a child from each of two marriages. My first wife was African American and my second wife was fully Jewish. My son was raised as African American from the beginning, and my mother cut herself off from him, her first grandchild, for the first two years of his life. Eventually, she accepted him. I believe we have to be tolerant, even if we do it out of self-interest; besides, it's the right thing to do. I appreciate your airing this; we must stand together against every form of oppression.

NOT THAT KIND OF PERSON

TRACY: I am a white middle-class woman, and it upsets me deeply when I watch television shows about Martin Luther King Jr. and how whites treated blacks. I change the channel and I see how we raped Native Americans of their land. I'm calling now because I don't want to be categorized as that kind of white person. I'd like to teach my children to look past color and see the soul; in the end, it's only me, God, and my soul.

CHAPTER TWENTY-TWO

Surrounded by Love in Billings

Murders, bombings, arson fires, and assaults are often considered page-one news; in fact, when newspaper editors select a story for page one, the message is, "We think this is most important." While the murders, fires, and corruption rate page-one treatment, there is another kind of story that I believe is also important news. It is the story of a town where citizens stood up for one another to protect the weakest among them. I first stumbled on the story buried in the back of my paper, under just a single-column headline.

The story said that a year earlier, in the city of Billings, Montana, flyers were circulated in mailboxes, on doorsteps, on car windows, spreading hate about Hispanics, gay and lesbian people, Indians, African Americans, and welfare recipients. The flyers were especially evil about the fifty Jewish families who call Billings their home. Ku Klux Klan material appeared on Martin Luther King Jr. Day, and then skinheads began appearing in small groups, glaring from the back pews of a black church in Billings.

The local police chief, Wayne Inman, was concerned about the pattern of hate in Billings. He had witnessed similar problems at his last job in Portland, Oregon, where hate caused a black man to be beaten to death with a baseball bat. Chief Inman knew where the Montana situation could lead and he said so. What happened next in Billings is news, make no mistake about it. According to the chief, the reaction by citizens was swift and unified. He told the *New York Times,* "There was community outrage saying, 'If you harass or intimidate one member of this community, you are attacking all of us.' " What he meant was that when swastikas and slurs were spray-painted on the home of a mixed-race couple, within several days roughly two dozen volunteers from Painters Local Union 1922 reportedly cleaned it up in forty-five minutes.

Rocks were thrown through the windows of the conductor of the Billings Symphony and, at another home, through the bedroom window of a five year old. Both houses had been decorated with Hanukkah menorahs. Jews' cars were smashed, bullets were shot through windows, and yet those intimidating incidents of hate inspired the people of Billings to take further action.

The Montana Church Association and local human rights groups encouraged non-Jewish people to put pictures of menorahs in their windows so that Jewish families celebrating Hanukkah could not be singled out. According to Marge McDonald of the Billings Church Association, "The non-Jewish homes, schools, and businesses that put up the menorahs and messages of support for the Jewish community started to find bullet holes or smashed car windows. What the community did was put up thousands more because the intimidation just outraged people."

The local newspaper twice ran a full-color, full-page drawing of a menorah and instructed citizens to cut it out and hang it up, which many people did. All over town, small businesses, like dry-cleaning outlets, began handing out thousands more of these paper menorahs.

What was lost in the news coverage about the Billings incident at the time is, I believe, something important—recognition of the diversity of the people who came forward to stand shoulder to shoulder with their Jewish neighbors and other hated groups on the list. Old and young people, couples, singles, country club members, and low-income citizens hung menorahs in their windows. And when these non-Jewish people received threats or saw their property damaged, it was a lesson. Marge McDonald said, "I can speak personally about this. It gave our family and our neighbors an understanding that we never could have had about what it feels like to be persecuted and faced with terrifying possibilities. Knowing that while you had the menorah up that a rock could be coming through your window was sobering to say the least."

I suspect that there were people in Billings who wanted to support the hated groups but were just too afraid. Wisely, Marge McDonald and many Jewish organizations told supportive but fearful people that it was the thought that counted. "Anyone who sincerely thought about putting up a religious symbol and felt that fear," McDonald said, "that is something they will never forget."

It would be gratifying to report that the hate groups disappeared from Billings in the face of so much community opposition, but that is not the case. Marge McDonald is proud that these groups are far more subdued and that the community is better equipped to deal with them in the future.

Perhaps this lesson learned from what happened in Billings will be the most enduring: simply ignoring hate literature and threats does not usually make them go away. "What this has done," McDonald added, "is help people learn that those who are targets of the hate movement need to be surrounded by our love and support in whatever way we can do it."

❦

I went on the air to talk with the listeners about Billings. "We live in an age when news editors believe that it is front-page news if a woman is attacked in a crowded city while frightened onlookers do nothing to some to her aid; but when the opposite response is true, when people in Billings, Montana, do come through for their neighbors, too many editors say that this is not a story for page one, this is a story for page thirty-eight, if it is a worthy story at all."

I think this is wrong of us in the news business. To

treat what is good as if it was separate from the news is the worst kind of news judgment. (The *New York Times* deserves credit for publishing a thorough magazine story on the Billings situation, though it initially ran the story about the incident on page thirty-eight.)

Because I believe that our acts of courage and compassion are every bit as newsworthy as hate, I invited listeners to call and tell me about a time in their lives when they stood up for someone who was vulnerable, or saw someone else who did.

Robert Leikind, head of the Connecticut chapter of the Anti-Defamation League, joined me in the studio to talk about times when he has seen people stand up for others. He told me that the Billings, Montana, response reminded him of what his mother described about growing up as a Jew in Germany. When she was eight or nine years old she heard Hitler on the radio saying over and over again, with utter contempt, "The Jews! The Jews!" It frightened her. The next day, when she went next door to play with her friend and constant companion, the girl's mother appeared at the front door, crying, and explained that she was no longer welcome at their home. "When I think of Billings," Leikind said, "I think of what courage can do to change events in a community."

Leikind also told his own story about an incident in his youth that inspired action in his later life.

ROBERT LEIKIND: When I was about ten, there was a boy in my class who was the kid who always got picked on. We'll call him Joe. It was always a very sad thing to see. One day a friend of mine and I were walking out of a classroom and we saw him crying by himself, and we sort of resolved between us that we were going to stick up for him from then on. The two of us took on his bullies, and actually turned the tide over a period of a few weeks by arguing with them and telling them to leave him alone. The reason this story came to mind was because years later I was working on a community development project in a rural, racially mixed part of Louisiana. On the day I have in mind we went into town and it happened that the local congressman was there, a guy by the name of Rorak, who had well-known credentials as a racist. We were walking through, and we obviously were not local people; he came up to us and knew who we were, and I can't repeat over the air what he said to us, but in a very unkind way what he said was, 'Why are you working down there where those black people live?' [He used the word *niggers*.] This was a congressman of the United States! That incident with the bullies when I was ten years old flashed through my mind and I just knew that we were doing the right thing and that's all that mattered.

❧

The listeners immediately responded to the theme of the show and demonstrated what I have sensed for so long, that the world is filled with people who believe in equality, though the news seldom reports their stories.

From the sound of the first woman's voice I guessed that she was perhaps in her seventies and well educated.

MURIEL: This is the first time I have ever called in to anybody's program but I had to tell you my story. I grew up in Tulsa, Oklahoma, and in 1923, when I was nine years old, they burned the whole Negro section of our town in one night. They claimed someone, a Negro, had insulted a white girl. What really happened was that a young man getting into an elevator tripped and fell against her. They were just looking for something. This burning of the town took place on the traditional maid's day off, which was on a Thursday. Ola, our maid, called my mother and said, "What shall we do? My sister and I are out with the children and they've burned our house!" My mother said, "Make your way as carefully as you can to our house and you'll stay with us until they find someplace for you to live." Then she gathered us around and she said, "Now, Ola's coming to live here and the neighbors might not like it. If they don't, we'll just put the furniture in front of the door." Well, Ola did come, and the neighbors didn't like it but they didn't do anything violent. All my life this incident was a pivotal thing. I'm now eighty-one and I have never stopped feeling indignant over injustice.

[I learned later in a note from her that she is Jewish and was in Austria from 1931 until 1936.]

LEIKIND: I think we underestimate in our own time how difficult it was for the mother of this caller to do what she did. I'm sure that in that period, when race hatred ran so deeply, it took enormous courage. I'm constantly impressed by the fact that the same things happen in our time, too. I received a call earlier this week from an education official at a school in Connecticut where there had been a series of anti-Semitic incidents. This person said to me that he wanted to take certain steps to address the problem, but that it was a difficult thing to do, not because people didn't think that there was a problem to address, but because they didn't want their community characterized in a certain way. When we got off the phone I realized that this was an unusual act of courage because this person's livelihood could be on the line. You make enemies. That's the kind of thing that I hear about daily.

❦

A caller, Paul, said he decided to make a point about bigotry at a health spa.

PAUL: This fellow, a very joyous guy, used to go around and tell jokes. I overheard him telling one using an ethnic slur. When he got done, I went over to him and put my arm around him and said, "You're a wonderful guy. You bring so much joy to people, but I was listening to your joke, and I know you didn't intend it, but somehow that ethnic bit in there was very painful. I think you can retell that joke in a way that doesn't hurt because I know you like to bring joy to people and you wouldn't hurt anyone." He looked at me aghast and apologized.

LEIKIND: One of the things that this points out is that the type of thing that happened in Billings is the type of thing that, in large and small ways, repeats itself over and over again in our lives. Paul's tactful way saved someone's dignity and at the same time helped resolve a painful situation.

MARYANN: This is a very small incident, simply a matter of verbal defense. One ordinarily thinks that bigotry stems from lack of education, but this incident occurred in New Canaan, Connecticut, which is a highly educated community. About fifteen years ago, my husband and I were taking the train from New Canaan into New York City. It was the days of the smoking cars. Two young black men were smoking in the no-smoking car, and an extremely well dressed white man spoke to them, using the word *nigger* constantly. He would announce to everyone, "Those niggers shouldn't be smoking in here," or, "Get those niggers out of here!" Everyone was sitting quietly, all beautifully dressed, and my husband said to the man, "I won't tolerate that kind of language." A number of people in the car turned to my husband and said, "This is a free country. We will say what we wish to say." I was so appalled. The conductor finally came into the car and asked the young men to leave because it wasn't the smoking car. The bad man was sitting directly in front of us and turned around and said to my husband, "What are you, some kind of a bleeding heart? You're dressed like one." I was trembling with anger. I'm usually a very quiet, gentle person, but as he stood up to get off the train, putting on his beautiful coat, I said to him, "A fine suit of clothes do not a gentleman make." Though he seemed to think of himself as a gentleman, he was so far removed from being a gentleman. I don't know how many people heard me, but I simply could not sit there and not say something. He just turned around and looked at me.

LEIKIND: Small acts of courage in some instances do as much for ourselves as they do for the people we're addressing because they become defining moments about where we stand and our courage to do what's right. It's one thing to step out when you know everybody is with you; it's another thing to step out when you're not so sure of that. That's real courage. I must say that we live in a wonderful state in a wonderful country where probably there's more respect for people with differences than most places in the world, but there's a lot of disrespect, too. We had a spokesperson from the Nation of Islam who was here and said some very horrible things. Many people in the community for whom it may not have been easy signed petitions, signed public letters, ranging from ministers, the bishop, to the leader of the NAACP, to clergymen of all colors and faiths. I think that took courage because this spokesman has a lot of popular support, and for people to stand up to it was not easy.

CLARICE: I had a house for sale in my neighborhood about three or four years ago and the people who were looking at it finally bought it. The neighbor on the other side called me one day and said, "Isn't it nice to know that it's a nice young couple from Newtown, and that means that there won't be any colored people moving into the neighborhood." I was shocked and speechless. I mumbled something and hung up and thought about it. I sat down and wrote her a letter about the Fourth of July, that my family goes back a long way; they came here from the other side in the 1700s. I said that I've been here a long time and I feel that the arms of this neighborhood, this town, this country, are open to anyone. I still don't have a relationship with this woman but at least I said what was on my mind. I have four children and we told them exactly where we stand and that we're willing to take our opinions outside our home.

LEIKIND: Talking to your children about your acts of courage is vital in ways that parents can hardly realize. Children follow their lead. When I was ten I had a grand-father in Paris I didn't see very often. My aunt, who was also living there, took me to a soup kitchen my grandfa-ther started to feed people who couldn't afford their own meals. He raised the money for it from a variety of sources. What I remember about it was when I walked in and I was introduced to somebody as his grandson. All of a sudden, these people started coming up to me to shake my hand, smiling. It never has left me, that image. I think in many ways it shaped my career and lifestyle choices. In our times, letting your children know that it's important to live with different people is an important message.

And if they don't get it, they may come up with other conclusions.

MAUREEN: There are many people in my city who are really doing their very best to have people of all kinds come together and be able to live together. I'd like to mention Bob Feltman, a Lutheran minister, because he helps the Regional Council of Churches sponsor a gay, lesbian, bisexual group called GEMS, which provides support and friendly visiting for older gay and lesbian people. I asked him one time, "Why are you so open about this? Why are you so tolerant and caring about other people?" He said that during the war he was on a train and there was an African American man standing between the cars, but the train was really lurching a lot. Some white man came by and said that he couldn't stand there and jostled him. Bob said that the African American man had been doing absolutely nothing, totally peaceful just standing on the train. That made such a big impression on him that that's what opened his mind and his heart to so many other things.

CONNIE: I'm at a gym; I don't know if there is too much background music. My story is also about a train. We were in college thirty-five years ago and went into New York City. We were headed back on the milk train so it made all these stops. There were a couple of people that were intoxicated and two very heavy women sitting across the aisle. These two men continued to very loudly embarrass them and make very derogatory remarks. We were sitting there saying, "We've got to do something!" So finally my husband stood up and said, "That's totally unnecessary. I want you to stop now." And they both did, but then they started slamming their fists and said to my husband, "We're going to get you, four-eyes." Fortunately, we just sat still and they got off shortly. I've always been proud of him for doing that, but I wonder if we would do that today with the frightful things that go on.

JAMES: I'd like to share a story with you which concerns a boarding school that I worked at for a time. I was hired as an adviser to students of color. At the time I was hired I didn't realize that I should have asked if they celebrated the Martin Luther King holiday. They did not, so I found myself in a real quandary as to what I should do as a person of color. I had to take stock and figure out what was the right thing to do. So after negotiating with administrators and after countless meetings with faculty, I decided to take a stand because I felt it was a very important issue. I decided to fast for a number of days until there was some sort of recognition on the campus. In doing so, I found that I put my position on the line, even though I had been brought in to bring about change. I found myself becoming a messenger and I couldn't stay. I had to provide the message and move on with my life. Subsequently the holiday was instituted at the academy; classes are suspended and students go about a day of activities centered around celebrating what Dr. King represented. This is one of the most prestigious boarding schools in the nation.

RON: About thirty years ago I was working for a large company and there was a chance for a promotion. I didn't get it and was naturally disappointed. I soon realized that the reason I didn't was because I'm gay. That motivated me at that point not to go into the corporate world, but to work hard and to get my own business, which I've had for about twenty-two years. Now when I hire somebody, particularly if they're black or Jewish or a woman, I make a point of telling them that under no circumstance is that a hindrance and they are to be treated properly and they are very much welcome in my company. Because of my background and because of the prejudice which I see quite often, I think it's made me a better boss and a better person and much more sensitive to prejudice. My trip is a little bit different perhaps than somebody else's, but I'm glad I'm gay. I think it's made me a much better person than I think I perhaps would have been if I had been born straight.

KIM: My issue is uncomfortable for most people. My boyfriend is from Iran. We've been together for five years and friends and family initially were very uncomfortable. People who didn't even know me would approach me and say, "Aren't you afraid?" I would say, "No, I'm not." He fled Iran during the Shah's reign. He was alone for sixteen years, and his religion is extremely mellow. He's not a terrorist or anything like that. I've been defending him for five years and at the same time educating people that not all Iranians and Middle Easterners have the same intent.

🌿

If examples of bigotry in the news represent significant numbers of people, perhaps examples of decency also reflect who we are.

CHAPTER TWENTY-THREE

Rebellion

In 1969, when I was in college, I joined a small group of students, black and white, to protest a move that we believed would limit the number of black students who would be admitted on scholarship. We staged a sit-in in Dean Betty Tipton's office, which she did not seem to mind, and after we received a great deal of press attention the trustees backed away from their proposal. It was my first "official" act of rebellion, and for every moment of exhilaration, we were anxious or afraid.

How much courage it must have taken for Rosa Parks to risk her safety, if not her life, by refusing a seat in the back of the bus.

Rebellion based on social conscience has a long, complex history. It is not rooted in any one political philosophy; it has given us our proudest moments, and it has broken our hearts.

The strict definition of rebellion is to defy authority or conventional behavior. I was interested to see what stories our listeners would tell about their small and big acts of rebellion. There was no shortage of calls.

MEET YOUR FATHER

Brian said it was his father who rebelled. "He taught me how to rebel. When I was three, we lived in Tuscaloosa, Alabama, and my father, who had returned from Germany and Russia during the war, was actually a stranger to me. One of our first experiences together was a bus ride we took in the company of the woman who helped my mother keep house. This woman was black; we were going home with her. We got on the bus in Alabama and the bus driver said, 'I'm sorry, she'll have to go to the back.' My father had me on his shoulders; he got on the bus, he looked at the bus driver and said, 'The hell she does; she's with me.' We proceeded to sit in the front of the bus and it was amazing, nobody said a word, absolute silence. The bus driver shut the door and drove and we all got off at my mother's helper's stop. My father never brought it up again, but that's how I learned.

"From that day on I never hesitated to rebel, and that was forty-two years ago. . . . [Voice cracks.] I am highly emotional when I speak about my father. My kids know all about him. They march to their own drummer, too."

THE EMPEROR'S CLOTHES

Sondra fought convention at her college. "I naively thought that the administration didn't know what was going on, and I behaved rather like the child who pointed out that the emperor has no clothes. For example, I went to a Catholic women's college and every Friday we had to stand in line for dating permission for the weekend. This could often take an hour of your time. You were supposed to tell the nun the name of the young man you were going out with, where you were going, what time you were going, etc. And what most of the girls did was have their mothers send in ten names at the beginning of the year; then a young boy adopted one of those names because if you met a young man on Wednesday and wanted to go out with him Saturday, there wasn't time to write home and get Mom to [submit his name]. So, one day I naively told the dean of women that we were all wasting our time standing in line, which they didn't appreciate, especially hearing that everyone was using this system. It didn't change anything and I was shocked that in a Catholic college they weren't interested in the truth. I had been paying my own way through college with scholarships and money I'd saved since I was fourteen. I also lived by myself; I considered myself an adult. A few years later, I told them that I was getting married between my junior and senior years, and they said, 'No, you can't because we don't have married students at St. Rose.' And I said, 'Oh yes you do; it's just that they keep it a secret.'

I found that hypocritical. In the fall I told them I was married; they said, 'Well, we're going to strip you of all your class privileges,' which they did. Then they turned to me and said, 'And, by the way, it's customary to invite the nuns to the wedding.' "

While I was amused by the expression I imagined on the nun's face, Sondra was not charmed. I understood why when I learned what a price she paid later on. She said, "I became pregnant and was going to do my student teaching senior year. Despite that I had the highest score from my high school on my scholarship exams they told me I could not do my practice teaching because 'We have never sent a pregnant girl out of St. Rose.' I said, 'In the first place, I'm married; second, these children see their mothers and aunts pregnant; it's silly.' But they were adamant about it; therefore, in my senior year I had to find another minor. When I graduated from St. Rose and wanted to get a teaching job, the St. Rose placement bureau told me they would not help because I hadn't done my practice teaching. We really needed my job at that point; my husband was still working on courses. I went on my own to a school in Troy, where the superintendent said he had a young man for the job who was certified while I was not. I said, 'If he's certified he's either a math major with an ed minor or a science major with an ed minor. I have both.' He laughed and hired me because it was true, I was more qualified without the practice teaching."

When I asked Sondra whether her acts of rebellion were part of her nature or surprising to her, she said, "I was always one to behave well. I did what I thought was right, not hypocritical. Standing alone at times helps to form your character."

EYES RIGHT

It was during World War II that Greg rebelled. "I was in Kelly Field, Texas. When they didn't know what to do with you in the air force, they marched you around, close-order drill, and it was really about as stupid an activity as you can imagine. I got so disgusted marching and marching mindlessly that I said to the fellow next to me, who felt the same way, 'When they take a right turn here, keep on walking straight and see what happens.' We did, and we continued to walk straight while the formation kept on going out to the drill field. They drilled in the dust and the sun while some of us went back to the barracks and had ourselves a little reading session. Later on, at another base, a fellow and I had been assigned to do KP and the KP sergeant was such an abusive guy that we said, 'Forget it!' We just walked out of KP and said we won't work for this guy. It was almost as though we were civilians."

FAITH: And what happened to you?

GREG: Nothing happened. They tried to find us but they really didn't know where we were. We were bright enough to say, "We will not tolerate this kind of foolishness."

Greg made me consider how anger is often a big part of rebellion, though I have known people who rebelled against the system with only fear as a companion, and that requires courage. When I asked Greg if he had acted as he did out of anger, he said, "I was angry. And to this day I don't know what would have happened had we been caught. We were future pilots. It was a matter of being fed up with the foolishness."

SYMPHONY IN SOCKS

I mentioned the topic of rebellion to a friend of mine who hiked up his pants and said, "You see this old brown belt? When I was playing in the Vermont Symphony Orchestra, fresh out of Juilliard School of Music, I would be all dressed up in my tuxedo, except that I would wear this old brown belt. It was my little act of rebellion against the formality. It looked completely ridiculous with the black suit but I did it anyway. I also took my shoes off and played in my black socks."

GOD'S NOT DONE

"*W*hen I was a teenager I rebelled against civilization," George said. "If people ate cooked foods, I ate raw hamburger, raw potato, raw eggs, raw everything. What I was supposed to do I refused to do."

Naturally, I wondered how George's parents reacted to his food rules but he didn't remember. When I asked if he was trying to find a way to set himself apart somehow, he said, "I'm still struggling with that. I'll learn someday; God hasn't finished with me yet."

During our show on rebellion, I had producer Diane Orson's permission to tell the story of Diane's eighteen-month-old daughter, Emily, who engaged in her first pointed act of rebellion against her parents. On occasion, Diane explained, when things were not going Emily's way, she would lean over and bite Diane or her father, Tim. "She would bite us on the arm, leg, or face, and let me tell you, it hurt!" Diane said. Eventually Diane and Tim managed to convince Emily there were other ways to express her frustration, but it was interesting to consider that children must be taught when they can and cannot be physical; the extraordinary amount of domestic violence tells me this is a lesson too many children never learned.

EYES LIKE SLITS

At the age of fifteen, Rashid stood up to his stepfather. "I don't recall ever having done anything wrong except the normal things that children do. But if I did anything he thought was wrong, he would close his eyes like slits, and I was petrified. He never laid a hand on me, but that look in his eyes absolutely froze me. One day, he did it to me and I said, 'You needn't bother doing that with your eyes. I will never be afraid of you again, or anyone else.' He never did it again."

When I asked Rashid what saying this had done for him, he answered, "It made me a much stronger person. I was never afraid of anyone again. After that, my father would look at me but he never tried that trick with his eyes because I would simply stare at him, and he would turn away."

Rashid told us that he now has children of his own. "I told all of them that they should never, ever be afraid of anyone, and they should always stand up for what they believe in. In fact, when my son Paul, who is now a doctor at the University of San Francisco, was in elementary school, he stood up for another little boy. He felt that the teacher was berating the boy. He simply said, 'I don't think that's fair.' He felt terrible about it, and that evening when I went into his bedroom to say good night to him, he was crying. He said, 'I think I'm going to be in trouble,' and he told me what happened. I went to school the next day and spoke to the teacher, who said, 'You know, I think we have a problem with Paul because he tends to cry easily.' And I said, 'Well, I'm not talking about that, I'm here to talk about his standing up for his fellow man. If everyone did, I don't think there would be wars, do you?' He looked at me, raised an eyebrow, and that was that."

REFUSING VIETNAM

For a caller named Dave, a serious act of rebellion occurred in 1968, and much was at stake—his freedom and his sanity. Here is our exchange just as it happened on the air that day:

DAVE: When I was in the U.S. Navy during Vietnam, the more I read about the war the more it started to disturb me. I kept thinking, how can I stand this; how can I stay? A friend at Bowling Green University during the Kent State [shooting of students by the National Guard] sent me something in the mail. I knew if I took this stuff I could either end up in the brig with a discharge or go absolutely nuts. I did it anyway and I ended up leaving the service.

FAITH: What did he send you in the mail?

DAVE: Mescaline.

FAITH: Oh, I see. You took this drug?

DAVE: Yes, I did, not to get high, believe me. I'd never taken it before in my life; I was terrified of it. I just did it because I felt I had to do something as an act of rebellion, as a way of dealing with it.

FAITH: And what happened?

DAVE: They ended up taking me to the base hospital, but just before that I sent some letters to [Connecticut] Senator Abraham Ribicoff and Mendell Rivers. The senator from Texas was sent down because there were some other things going on; we had racial riots at the base.

They wanted to investigate the whole thing. They ended up discharging me.

FAITH: Honorably?

DAVE: Yes.

FAITH: Obviously, you never went to Vietnam. What do you think about it now?

DAVE: It affected my life forever; it changed the way I see the world. You can't go back. It changed the way I saw authority, and I realized that your own life is not that important; it's more important to follow through on your ideals. I still deal with things on the same level; I try to live it the way I see it.

FAITH: Have you rebelled since then against other things that you felt weren't right?

DAVE: My rebellion is a little more quiet. I put on quite a show for that 1968 rebellion. I said everything I had to say about the war to five lieutenants and I don't know how many doctors; they grilled me until two in the morning. It was pretty intense. They threatened to arrest me; I had to go with them down to sick bay. It went on and on and on for months until I left.

FAITH: For some people, especially those who face frequent discrimination simply because of who they are, the very act of getting up in the morning and facing each day is an act of courage. People who do not know your personal qualities see your existence as an affront.

EATING MONEY

I laughed when Martha called with her story. "When I was in college in Florida, I was on scholarship and so was the man I eventually married; we had been high school sweethearts. We had very limited allowances, and we would save up and save up, and every once in a while we would splurge on a candy bar from this one candy machine at the college. This machine kept eating all our money and not giving us any candy. We had quite a bulldog of a security man; in fact, he was a Wallenda—his children were the Flying Wallendas, the trapeze artists. We all loved this man very much. But eventually, the bad money-eating candy machine had its day. In the middle of the night, the boys put it on top of the physics building, facing the eastern Florida sun. The next morning all these Presbyterian college students were standing around just watching chocolate melt everywhere and, oh, it was a mess. We got a new candy machine and you'll never guess how it turned out. You would put your money in and the candy machine would spit out candy bar after candy bar for free!"

END OF THE LINE

*W*hen Jean graduated from high school in 1950, she went to work at the Aetna Life Insurance Company, where she was the youngest but not the dumbest member of the department. "We would figure out loans for people

who wanted to borrow money, which was a lot of arith-
metic. We would do our papers and pass them on; if they
were wrong they would give them back to us. I was no
better or worse than anyone else but my pile to correct
kept getting bigger. So I said to the boss I didn't think
they were all my papers, and he said, 'Sure they are.' I
noticed that all the older people were putting theirs on
mine and, being young, they didn't expect me to speak
up. So one day I took all the papers and I went to my
boss and threw them at him. I said, 'Here, I'm not doing
this anymore.' I put on my hat and coat and went home.
My mother yelled at me, my father yelled at me, everybody yelled at me. I got a telephone call from my boss;
he told me to come to work the next day, and nothing
ever happened. When I think back to it now, I wonder
how in the world I did that. I learned that if I didn't stick
up for myself no one else would."

THE SHRINK LAUGHED

"This is a doozy," Bernadette said. "In 1955, I entered the convent right out of high school. I was in the
convent for fifteen years and I was a real honeybunch. A
lot of things happened through all these years and I just
accepted them. In the fifteenth year I was transferred to
teach at Mary Louis Academy, where I graduated from. In
that high school there was a person, a chemistry teacher, I
admired greatly. One day, late in the afternoon, I needed
a chemical and I went into this person's room, where all

the chemicals were kept, and I left a note saying I would return it tomorrow. I went over to the convent and I met this person in the hall; she was absolutely livid. She's about six inches taller than me and bombastic. She said, 'How dare you take my chemicals?' At that moment it was as if lightning struck me. I walked upstairs to the superior's room, knocked on the door, and said, 'I have something to say to you and I have to say it now.' I pushed open the door, walked in, and sat down. 'Whatever it takes,' I said, 'I'm leaving. Get me the papers, I'll give you two weeks.' I walked out, that was it. Because this was so unlike me, they sent me to a psychiatrist in New York, who laughed. He said, 'There's nothing wrong with you.' I said, 'Look, what happened to me was that I saw myself in her place. She had changed [from when I first knew her] and I figured there was no future in this.' I had had the last insult to what I thought was a noble calling. I've never gotten married; I've been a teacher for thirty-five years, still going strong, and I love it."

Bernadette fits into the "Last Straw" category of rebellion—you have no idea you're going to blow until you do.

"I haven't entered a church since that day," Bernadette added. "I can't deal with the way they tell you to live your life."

BAREFOOT BRIDE

Mary called to tell me about a minirebellion at her own wedding. "My idea of a wedding was to be somewhere barefoot out on a craggy beach with a full moon and my husband; seagulls as attendants and that's it. Unfortunately, we both come from very large Italian families and that wasn't going to happen. I ended up with a white dress and a big church, orchestra, choir, the whole works. We were standing at the altar [at the end of the ceremony] and just before we [walked back down the aisle] I kicked my shoes off and left them on the altar; I walked down the aisle barefoot! The photographer got a very nice shot of my feet peeking out from under my gown. Little by little people began to realize that my shoes were on the altar. Most of my friends know I'm a beach bum anyway and didn't think strangely of it. Some of the groom's family were a little rattled by it. The most rattled was my poor mother; she thought I had done it to ruin my wedding. I said, 'But Mom, I didn't do it walking UP the aisle, I did it walking DOWN the aisle!' I thought it would be over and done with that day but the photographer has a window showcase on Main Street in my parents' town and he chose to put that particular picture on display because I looked so happy and comfortable. Unfortunately for my mother, not only are my toes showing, but so is my little silver toe ring."

I asked Mary what she thinks of when she looks

at that picture now. "I just feel happy because at that point in the wedding the tension was over. I was married to this wonderful man. Our lives were just beginning. And I got to get out of those tight little white shoes."

CHAPTER TWENTY-FOUR

Inside Alcoholics Anonymous

If you are not a member of Alcoholics Anonymous, you are about to read something rare—the testimony of members of AA told word for word in their own voices.

Under the careful supervision of the state AA public information committee, we began having Alcoholics Anonymous gatherings on my show in 1989. Since AA is mysterious to nonmembers like myself, and most AA meetings are closed to outsiders, our AA shows provide a unique opportunity to experience the textures of interaction that have proven so valuable to the two million members of this anonymous organization.

I have now met hundreds of alcoholics who had lost much of what was dear to them—family, friends, and career—and then transformed themselves by working hard to live by AA's Twelve Step Program. One thing not commonly understood about Alcoholics Anonymous and its Twelve Steps is that they encourage and strengthen good character in those who regularly use them.

The stories I hear from AA members in the studio and those who phone in make great radio; they also document remarkable courage and demonstrate that change and recovery are truly possible. But I am also supportive of AA for personal reasons—I find myself wondering if AA could have helped my own mother and father, who died drunk when I was a sophomore in high school. Unfortunately, I knew nothing of the AA program, nor of Al-Anon and Alateen, for relatives and friends. Living with my parents while they suffered from this disease was horrible. They were isolated and so was I. I know now that twenty-three million Americans are affected by alcohol and drug addiction. I find it peculiar that the government does not embrace AA on the basis of public health alone, especially considering AA's track record worldwide. Is there some other leaderless program that has helped two million people transform their lives, as AA has done, free of charge?

Like most people who do not have a drinking problem, I had no idea what an AA meeting was like or why it worked. I sat there fascinated as I heard AA members explain with natural eloquence what they had lost at the hands of this disease, and what they had gained in sobriety. I realized that the familiar, frequently used slogans AA members repeat, like "One day at a time," are shorthand principles that also enable members to attend a meeting anywhere in the world and know what's going on. I saw that members usually introduce themselves at meetings by stating their first names and the line, "and I'm an alcoholic." The repetitive identification with alcoholism is helpful, especially since it is easy to fool yourself into thinking that you are finally cured—alcoholism, AA members tell us, is a cunning, baffling, and powerful disease.

Attending a number of AA meetings—they're held in church basements, community centers, libraries—I found gatherings of people from all professions, and of differing ages, orientations, and races, who had come together to tell their own stories simply because doing so helps them stay sober. AA members with good sobriety understand the notion of putting their faith in something greater than themselves, whatever that might be. (Meetings are strictly nondenominational despite the use of the word *God*.)

Because of my respect for AA, I was interested in finding a way to expose both its simplicity and complexity to a wider audience, without violating the program's traditions, including anonymity, which is crucial to its success. The chance to do that came about seven years ago, when I teamed up with two AA members, Norm A. and Louise A., to "show" rather than "describe" the program. I agreed to serve as radio host and occasional interviewer for once-a-month AA open public information gatherings broadcast live from our New Haven studio. Several AA members joined us in the studio each time to tell their stories during prime time. Besides the showcase we offer, there is another unique aspect to our radio shows; apparently, no one had ever thought to invite people to join such an event by telephone from wherever they were—home, car, office, or pay phone. Many AA members say they cannot believe that they can now participate while caught in rush-hour traffic, or while they are housebound with illness, child care, or transportation problems.

To tell the truth, I didn't know what our general listeners would think of this experiment, and the last thing I wanted to convey to them was the mistaken idea that AA or we were trying to say that no one should drink. (AA's principles say nothing of the kind.) I soon realized that the chance to get a glimpse of AA's traditions and hear members tell their dramatic stories was fascinating to nonalcoholics.

Word of our radio shows started to spread through a small story in the national AA newsletter, *The Grapevine*. The *New York Times* did a small feature on us and our phones began ringing with inquiries. Among the callers was one of my favorite reporters, Linda Ellerbee, who filmed our radio AA show for her television special, which airs on HBO in 1996, on the many ways to recover from drug and alcohol addiction. The director of Connecticut's Alcohol and Drug Abuse Commission sent us a letter saying, "The radio meetings are the most creative communications strategy I have ever encountered in the alcohol and drug field. It brings what is too often our secret problem into the public light, while preserving both people's anonymity and the intensely personal quality of addiction."

Perhaps one day we will be able to offer our AA meetings to a national or international audience. Meanwhile, the Connecticut Department of Mental Health and Addiction Services has helped cover some distribution costs with annual grants from the state fund of money confiscated from drug dealers. (Each radio gathering begins with the disclaimer that AA does not endorse any sponsor of the show or the station.)

I am delighted when callers say that after listening to our AA shows they decided to go to their first meeting, or when alcoholics say that now they have returned to AA meetings after a long absence and that listening to the radio program has helped them make that decision.

The callers participating in these radio AA shows have told many moving stories, though one is especially memorable. A man named John, who was in our studio with Norm and Louise, explained how he had deteriorated physically and mentally from alcoholism until he lost everything. AA helped him save his own life. I asked John if he had ever tried to convey to his ten-year-old son why he goes to AA. He said he hadn't, though occasionally he does bring him along to meetings. When I began taking calls from listeners, I punched a button at random; I suddenly heard a young boy say hello, and I knew from the startled look on John's face who it was. Amazingly, his son had gotten through our jammed switchboard. The boy said, "I just wanted to say thanks, Dad." There was silence (and tears) in the studio after John's son hung up.

The stories presented here provide an unusual opportunity to glimpse how AA's Twelve Step approach saves lives. In all my years of interviewing and reporting, I can say that working on the AA story is one of the most remarkable experiences I have had. I like to think that my mother and father are somewhere listening.

(Note: Most AA members begin their testimony by introducing themselves and saying, "and I'm an alcoholic." The frequent identification is a helpful reminder of the problem.)

WHAT JOY HAVE YOU DISCOVERED IN SOBRIETY?

BOB: During the time that I was actively drinking, I was so self-absorbed that I wasn't too conscious of the glories of nature or the pleasures of life. After I had been in AA for perhaps six months, I just woke up one morning and I could hear the birds sing. I hadn't noticed this sound for years. I also began to be interested in health. I had come to nearly the end of my life from our disease. I was in the hospital with cirrhosis and massive esophageal hemorrhaging and nearly died. And then early in sobriety, slowly, I began to realize that I missed skiing. I began running. I started appreciating all of the different seasons of the year. As a drinking alcoholic working in New York and going in on the train, I just hated winter! It was cold and wet, you got splashed by the cabs, and you wore clothes that you didn't want to wear. After I had sobered up I became more interested in getting out in the air in every season, and I began to find that winter, lo and behold, was my favorite season! Now in my thirty-first year of sobriety, which is joyous indeed, I live half the year in Sun Valley, Idaho. Although I'm seventy-five years old, I'm still an avid skier and runner.

CINDY: I can't wait to get into my car and listen to this meeting every month. I've been sober ten months only; it was the same experience for me. All of a sudden one day I went and I sat in a field and I started looking around at the sky and everything. I thought, God, this is wonderful. I have to tell you, a year ago I couldn't have sat by myself for more than five minutes without panic or distress. Sobriety has given me that, and it's the most wonderful thing in the world.

LOUISE: When I first came to AA there was nothing joyous in my life. I was more numb than anything else. I remember I stopped drinking in May, and I came into the fellowship of AA in August. I'll never forget that day. It was October 19, 1976. I pulled the shades up to look outside and it absolutely hit me what a gorgeous day it was. It was like the first time I had ever seen the sun, the first time I had ever seen a blue sky. I was reminded of that just the other day, driving my son to work. You go up over a rise and you look out over a city. The sky was perfectly clear and you could see all of the buildings. My life does not always go the way I want it, but living life for me today is a joy. I'll sit and complain about it, but I'm just so grateful to be in reality.

TIM: I'm a newcomer to AA, just about three months. I am one of the lucky few who got to experience joy very early on. I think that AA is one of the world's best-kept secrets. Alcoholics mess up their lives in particularly bad order, so we need these lessons perhaps more than people who have good coping skills. Learning how to live in the moment and appreciate things instead of finding fault brings joy to everything. I have learned how to shut off the noise in my head. They call it "stinking thinking" in the program. Like others, I have found joy in the outdoors. Even in things I used to hate, like standing in line, I can now find a peaceful moment. I turn around and chat with the person behind me. Working in my office, which I used to hate . . . definitely joy there. The Twelve Steps are a program for everybody, not just alcoholics.

BOB: I've always been interested in the fact that before AA was ever here, when people just didn't know what to do with alcoholics, there were many so-called cures for alcoholism, places to send people. The alcoholics would go there for a few weeks. The emphasis was always on getting the alcoholic to stop drinking. So he would stop drinking while he was in the cure place, but as soon as he got out he always went back to drinking because until AA came along there was never any emphasis on how to handle sobriety. That's really what the principles and the Twelve Steps are all about.

ROBERT: I was a very, very sick person. I had been a daily drinker for about twenty-five years and always went to work and showed up for social occasions. Many people didn't realize that what was wrong with me was alcoholism. I was a hidden drunk in many ways. But it was getting to me physically; it nearly killed me. Finally, I just made such a spectacle of myself in the eyes of the people all around me that I was thrown into a drunk farm. It was really there that I found AA. The people who came there from AA shared their experience, strength, and hope with me. For a while I was marking time until someone discovered the magic pill which would enable me to drink without killing myself, hurting my family, and losing my job. But about six months into the program I had an awakening one evening. My wife was having an evening cocktail, we all did in those days. I would have a fruit juice, and she said, as she had many times before, "Sweetie, it's just so sad that you can't have a drink with me, and you're so good to do this." I said, "Sit down, I want to tell you something." I said, "If that magic pill were invented tomorrow and I could go back to drinking without any ill effects on my health or job or family or anything, I wouldn't be interested." And this was a new thought to me! Suddenly the whole desire to drink had been miraculously lifted. It was either due to the grace of God or to the fact that the AA program had been rubbing off on me. I choose to think it was the grace of God that enabled me to "come to" at that moment. I never have had a desire to drink since.

JOE: Hi, my name is Joe, twenty-eight and a half years sober. I like what he said, that he came into the program reluctantly. I always say one thing: There is a future in the past. I'm glad I'm an alcoholic because without it and AA I would have never grown the way I think I've grown. And I wouldn't value the things that should be valued, like family, grandchildren, self-esteem, health, all the good things of life. My joy comes from waking up in the morning and not reaching inside the pillowcase for the bottle, which I did repeatedly as a round-the-clock drinker. Now I go downstairs and punch up the coffeepot. When I'm through dressing, the coffee's ready. That's a joy to me, to drink that cup of coffee in the morning and know that my head is clear and I feel good and I'm on my way to work. I have to get up at 2:45 in the morning for the work that I do. I can remember that I was so weak when I drank in Pensacola, Florida, that I stopped the Volkswagen in the middle of traffic because I had no strength to shift the gears. I had five hospitalizations with DTs. The only thing I can remember before I went to the hospital for the last time is sitting in a bar out on Long Island, ordering a rum and Coke at eight in the morning. I could see workers passing the barroom and walking with cups of coffee, and I said, "That's what I want to do. I don't want to be here." My original sponsor, who is still around, led me to the AA program thirty years ago. It took me a couple of years to finally get it; I knew it was a gateway, but I just didn't know how to get in. I wouldn't let myself do it. I think I fought it every step of the way. When I went to a meeting and somebody put out their hand and said, "How are you?" they were genuinely interested in how you felt and how you were doing. I thought they were intruding upon my privacy, and I got very angry. I'd hide in the corner of the room or sit in the back. Today I find myself more outgoing than I've ever been, not afraid to go to a party with my wife. I finally found out after all these years that my wife is the best friend I have. We're invited to a number of things, but I keep events that expose me to a lot of alcohol to a minimum. I only have one other thought, that the greatest joy I have is spending three or four afternoons a week with my two granddaughters, four and a half and two years old. That would not have been possible had I not put the cork in the bottle.

MARY: It was funny that this show should be on as I was driving in my car. I stopped to get the mail and in the mail was a card from my sister, who has been an alcoholic for some thirty or forty years. I know this is about joy, but I hear you all laughing and seemingly sober and happy, and I wonder how you can get to someone like my sister, who heaps pain and sadness on her family and has done so for thirty years. How do you get to that person? She's been to drunk tanks and sobered up for a few weeks at a time. She's lost everything, her family, her friends, her belongings. She's a very cruel person, and although it would be easy to just ignore her, you want somehow to get to her. I really don't know how to do it.

BOB: I don't know any answer to it either. It is such an enigma that denial of the disease is a symptom of the disease. We don't have much influence on other people, and particularly on our relatives. I have never been successful in trying to get anybody into AA who wasn't so desperate that they finally wanted to come themselves. No, AA traditionally doesn't proselytize, doesn't go out and try to get members. We are just a society of recovered alcoholics, and we remain that. I don't know any way to reach a person like that unless there is somebody in AA who is close to her, and finally she has the desire to have the kind of joy in living that that person has. You can't really induce that. Don't give up. I knew one person who came into AA when he was about eighty-four years old, and he's had a wonderful life for the last ten years, so it can happen.

FRAN: This is the first time I've heard about this show, and I'm at work. I've had a great day, but I'm tired, and when I'm tired and I know I need a meeting . . . oh, thank you so much. I don't have very long in the program, three years in November. I think it's fantastic. I feel great. I never "felt" before I got into the program. I was always afraid, introverted, isolated. And here I am talking to I don't know how many people on the radio and I don't care because if I get my message across to one person, then I would be happy. Three years ago I was sitting at this same phone, calling a suicide hot line, that's how serious things were. I didn't want to be anymore. AA is a program for living. I didn't have a clue as to how to live or what to do, and I was negative. AA turned around my brain, from illness to well-being, and I gained a spirituality; that combination is what keeps me going.

BOB: I wanted to tell the last caller about my friend Cubby, who came to us from California. He was a terrible alcoholic and heroin addict. He spent the last several months of his drinking sitting in a chair, shooting heroin and drinking brandy, completely isolated from the world and nearly dying. Finally he came to AA. He lived out in the seedier part of Los Angeles, and he was out walking on the streets after he had been in AA for a little while. He had this funny sensation come over all of his body and his thinking, and he was scared because he thought he might be going into some sort of a seizure. So he went to a phone and he called his AA sponsor and he described his feelings and asked his sponsor, "What do you think?" His sponsor thought for a minute, and he said, "Well, in my experience, it seems to me that what you're describing is called happiness."

JOHN: I'm an Al-Anon member. I've recently separated from my wife, who was the alcoholic. What prompted my call was the woman that called in about her sister. You can't do anything about your sister, but you can sure help yourself a lot, and that's what Al-Anon is all about. I was unable to see my children today, so I was very, very depressed driving home, and just as I came across the border, I picked up your show. I was really thrilled to hear this because I, too, was expecting to pull open my little book and start looking for a meeting tonight.

STUART: I can relate on both sides of the fence because I grew up in an alcoholic household. I'm in Al-Anon because I married an alcoholic. It's almost as if I've gone back to that joyous, wonderful person that I was when I was very small before all the family problems came in. Going to AA also gave me a warm feeling because other people believed in me. It would take me forever to give thanks for what I have today.

HOW WERE YOU TREATED AS A NEWCOMER IN AA?

CLAIRE: It seemed to me when I came to AA that the room was full of light, people seemed so happy. There was this big, burly guy and they had a cake for him with one candle on it. It was his one-year AA anniversary. He was talking about taking the time to smell the roses. This guy looked like Ferdinand the Bull. I couldn't imagine who these people were. Everyone looked right at me to speak to me. I couldn't look anybody in the eye without dark glasses on. People gave me their phone numbers. I had to go up to somebody and say, "I don't know how to stop drinking." They weren't crowding me in any way. I would call these numbers they gave me because I couldn't go to treatment. I was clinically paranoid and I was so frightened. I had to stay at home and do it. It wasn't fun.

If I had it to do over, boy, I'd go right into treatment. At that first AA meeting they also gave me what they call a Surrender Chip, which is a custom in some meetings. It was just a regular poker chip. Somebody taped a dime to it and said, "If you ever think you're going to have a drink, call me and use this dime." So that was nice. I could get these really simple ideas. I kept the poker chip in my pocket.

BARBARA: Yes, I do remember being a newcomer. When I was miserable and desperate and called the AA number in the phone book, it took three days for anybody to reply. Now I understand why that was, but I didn't then. Like everyone else has said, I was scared to death. A gentleman called me and asked if I could get there alone or could he come and get me. I did get there alone. I didn't know what alcoholism was. I did not know what was wrong with me, I just knew I was totally miserable and my life was getting more and more of a mess. When I got there, there was a lady there who had been in the program for a number of years. This was back in 1957; there were very few women in the program then. It took me years to learn that the reason it took them three days to answer me was they had to spend that time finding another woman to be a speaker at the meeting. She told her story of what had happened to her. She'd lost her children, her family, everything. She was waking up in strange cities not knowing how she got there. And what she told me that night was where I was going if I kept on the way I was. I began to understand for the first

254 ¼ *FAITH MIDDLETON*

time that it was a disease, alcoholism was, and that there was something that could be done about it. I never saw that woman again. I wish someday to thank her, but I can't. The men who were in the program were from skid row. They were men who were miracles, really. Some of them had last rites two or three times and had survived. They made me welcome even though I'd had a much higher "bottom" than theirs. They never treated me as if I were an intruder. They always served pie and I didn't have to serve it, which was a treat. I didn't have to clean up the coffee either, until later when things got better and it was fun to do it. AA was marvelous from the beginning. They told me things, that I didn't have to do anything at all, which was good because if you tell me I have to do it, I'll do something else. There was no money involved. I didn't have to pay a lot; it was a quarter at every meeting and that I could manage. I didn't have to get dressed up. I didn't have to put my lipstick on straight or worry about whether my hair was combed, which was the plague of my life when I was drinking. It was just a marvelous place to be and they were a bunch of guys with wonderful senses of humor, and day after day, week after week, I stayed sober one day at a time just so I wouldn't disappoint them.

WHEN DID YOU FIRST FEEL HOPE?

PAUL: I decided AA wasn't for me because I had these preconceived ideas of what an alcoholic is. I thought it was a person who drank every day and always needed a drink; I didn't drink like that. I was a binge drinker on weekends, and I got in trouble with it, but I really didn't think alcohol was the problem. The third and hopefully the last time I came to AA was back in 1984. My attitude was, I'm going to prove once and for all that I really don't have this problem. Once I surrendered my judgment and just did the things that were suggested in there, none of which were very hard but were things I didn't want to do, I just kind of bit the bullet and did it. And here we are some ten years later, and there's no doubt in my mind about my alcoholism. It was the greatest move I ever made in my life. I just had to learn to turn off big brain and listen. In AA we learn that it's not just a drinking problem, we have a thinking problem.

MARK: When I first came to AA four years ago, I was, basically, living on the streets and probably about sixty pounds heavier than I am now, with open sores, and I was pretty insane from using drugs and alcohol. I walked into my first meeting on a Saturday morning and I was pretty gone. Someone mentioned in the meeting about picking up their first drink in sixth grade, and a flash went off in my head. For the first time I identified. And it was the first time I felt I could identify the problems I had with something, and realize that other people around me had the same problems and that there was help. My mind opened my mind to a whole avenue of ideas about alcohol, drugs, shame, self-hatred. I was closed down, and I had no ability to keep myself open until I walked into that first meeting. I was living in a shelter, I was separated at the time, and I was going down fast. I started going to three meetings a day. It completely changed my outlook. I'm still married, I have a son now, almost four. I have a really good job, and I sponsor two people. I had a slip about two and a half years ago which, in one day, put me back on the streets down in Manhattan. I almost over-dosed on vodka and cocaine, and I got right back into the program. I called up my sponsor and got right on a train and came back to Connecticut. I've been through a lot of hard times; we lost a daughter, I lost my father when I was in the program, but I never ran from those problems, I kept facing them. And if I didn't have the support of AA, I wouldn't be here today. No matter how far down you go and no matter where you are it always gets better, if you just keep going to meetings. Even if you don't have the willingness to change, you change. And you don't even know it sometimes, until you suddenly look back.

HOW DO YOU STAY SOBER?

AMALIA: When I found out that I was an alcoholic, the first thing that I learned was the fact that alcoholism is an illness. When I was in treatment, the medicine that they prescribed for me was to go to AA meetings to stay sober. I have realized that I have to take what I learn in those meetings and practice those principles in all my affairs. That's not easy, but I try and that's what keeps me going. I also try to get involved in service work. Coming to this studio for this radio meeting is part of doing service work, just to let other people know that there is a way to stay sober.

DAVID: It's just wonderful to be driving home from work and hear this happening on the air. What I do to stay sober is I go to regular meetings. I do three meetings a week. I've been sober a long time, so I'm down to three meetings a week, but I'm real steady and regular with them, and I go even when I don't feel like it, not because I might drink but because I won't see those people again that I've grown to really care for. I continue working on the Twelve Steps. Some of them I'll never be able to accomplish perfectly, but I need to continue working on them.

BETSY: I'm a fellow recovering alcoholic and addict. I'm nervous because I never called into this thing before but . . . I've been sober for about a year and a half. I'm still in high school, so it's very hard for me to keep sober. I've had to change all my friends. What I've learned is not to compromise my principles, you know, go back to the old people. I have to keep my life really simple. I do fun things, like go bowling. Before, I'd have to drink just to do anything. It's so good. My family is really active in AA. My parents told me about this meeting. They listen to this station all the time, to the classical music. I don't particularly like the music.

WHAT IS THE VALUE OF ANONYMITY?

NORM: Anonymity is the secret of sobriety. Before I quit drinking, I wanted my persona to be recognized by everybody and I had these great opinions that people should know. I was what Bill Wilson, AA's cofounder, used to call the "power driver." I wanted you to believe what I believed in. I looked at people for what they could do for me, not what I could do for them. Coming into AA, I've become part of a group, so we have a group conscience.

LOUISE: When I go to the doctor I have no problem letting them know that I'm an alcoholic. That's more for my benefit than theirs. They know how to deal with me better. I don't consider that an anonymity break. On the radio show here, I'm just Louise, and I don't have to give my last name at this level. Yet when I go to my home group, I want everybody to know my last name so that they can get in touch with me. If the members of my home group don't know how to get in touch with me, then how can I perform my primary task of helping other people get sober and stay sober? Each area of my life is ruled by anonymity in one form or another.

HAROLD: It is a mystery that people do stay sober. To try to explain this mystery and miracle to people on the outside is difficult. It's extremely important to be anonymous. We only break the anonymity when we're helping another drunk or alcoholic. We say, "In order to keep it, you have to give it away," so when people come in, I will give my number. I don't give my number out indiscriminately, especially to somebody who's still drinking and hasn't got a clue that they're having a problem. I don't go around looking for drunks to get them sober, believe me! I just wait, or I give my number to the parish priest.

CALLER: Hi. This is the first time I'm calling you. I get out of work about this time, and this is the fifth time I've heard your program. I was arrested for drunk driving a while back, and the counselor told me that I had a problem with drinking. I told him that I really didn't think I did, but if I ever thought it got out of hand I would try to do something about it. He suggested AA. It has been getting out of hand lately, and I'm really confused about how to go about this because I'm sort of scared to make a commitment to something I really don't know too much about. You were talking about spirituality and about how religion isn't really pushed upon you in AA, and I guess that's true, but my problem is that I don't even believe in God at all. I really think I have a problem and I really think I should go to a meeting, but I have no idea how to get information about it or anything.

NORM: The only requirement for membership is the desire to stop drinking. Nothing else is required of you. Many of us have been antisocial and uncomfortable in groups, and yet you come into AA and you will feel welcome and feel at ease. It happened to me. If you just look in your phone book in whatever town you're in, you'll see Alcoholics Anonymous. Call that number and say you'd like to find out where a meeting is near you, and they will tell you. You can even ask somebody to phone you from AA if you'd like to have a personal discussion with somebody before you go to a meeting. I watch newcomers come in and I think they are impressed with our traditions. We don't bug anybody; we have leaders but no bosses. Nobody's going to give you a bad time or be judgmental of you. You're going to find a new freedom and a new happiness that you've never been able to find anywhere else. It's worth taking a look. We have many atheists and agnostics in AA. It's not a requirement that you believe in anything other than you think maybe the group can help you. That's a higher power.

PEARL: I found AA when I was really down and I had hit my bottom. I was married for thirty-eight years to an alcoholic, and he died of alcoholism, and he was going to AA. He would come home from his AA meetings and buy his bottle. He said that he didn't belong there. I said that that was never going to happen to me, but within two years I was calling AA and begging to come into those rooms because five days before I called AA I sat in the middle of my kitchen and screamed, "God, why don't you let me die? What are you saving me for!" I was totally wrecked, despaired, broken, and in those days a woman who drank was a tramp, a loose woman, and was totally no good, so I figured that was it. I was working second shift, and I would have to have a couple before I went to work and then have some when I came home, and finally it was around the clock. The reason I found out I was really in trouble, I thought I was doing my job all right and my boss sent me home one night. I said, "I've been worse than this." And that was it. I didn't drink for five days, and I called AA. From then on, my life has been wonderful. I've had my ups and downs, but I know now I can't blame anyone, the kids, family, friends, anybody. I was the one who drank, and the alcohol didn't reach out to me, I reached out to it. I've been sober thirteen years. As you said, you go in and they accept you for what you are.

TOM: The reason I'm calling is that I have been in and out of AA for a number of years. The last meeting I went to was approximately two years ago, and as always, I ended up drinking again. My statement is that I want to go to an AA meeting but I feel like an absolute failure. I believe it says somewhere in the text of AA that there are some of us who do not make it, and I've had more slips than I care to count. I feel very much ashamed going back and having to say that. I've tried doing it on my own. I listen to this program the first Monday of every month. Thank God you're there because it does help me. I just wanted to make that statement. Thank you.

NORM: You would be so welcome, and you're not the only one that's come to AA and gone back out and drank again. If you had a meeting of thirty people and you asked people who went out and drank again to raise their hands, you'd probably have more than half of them raise their hands. We have a disease that's alcoholism, and we come here finally when we state what you're saying, that you feel powerless over alcohol. Come back in and be welcome.

CLAIRE: I was touched by the guy just calling in saying that he was afraid to go back to meetings and felt like a failure. I know the line in the Big Book that he's talking about, that some people don't make it because they're not capable of being honest with themselves. I was really afraid I was one of those people. I sat there thinking, yeah I'm the one who doesn't make it. The line that I wanted to offer him is the first line in AA, "Rarely have we seen a person fail who has thoroughly followed our path." I really hung on to that. I felt like I was doing the very best that I could with what was being given to me in the meetings and using what I could make use of, and if I did that, it would have to be very rare for me not to make it. And I did make it! I've been sober for twelve years now. I really don't know anybody who works the AA program that it doesn't work for. I like to say that when I came into AA I was dying of terminal uniqueness. I thought there was nobody like me. I was not convinced that drinking was my problem; I thought I was crazy. It did seem to me that trying to quit drinking was worth a shot and that it might make a big difference for me. I guess I always dreamed that there would be some moment in my life when I would say, "Well, this is the moment when my life turned around," and really the day I came to AA was the day that happened. I found out that I am unique, but I'm only as unique as everybody else in the room.

PASSING ON YOUR SOBRIETY
TO ANOTHER PERSON

ROB: I had my first drunk when I was fourteen; the drinks felt warm and wonderful going down, I went into a blackout, woke up the next day nauseous, and thought it was the most wonderful experience I had ever had. I discovered drinking allowed me to do social things that I had always been afraid of, calling girls, asking someone to dance. I went through my adult life with all kinds of problems, had several marriages and businesses that failed, never realizing that maybe alcohol was the problem. I had reached a point where I was alone, barely hanging on to a job. Physically, I was very ill, extremely overweight, bloated, enlarged liver, poor circulation. I remember coming home from work one day and there was nothing bad particularly that had happened. Life in general was lousy, so it was just a typical day for me. I had been drinking all day. I walked into my living room. I remember falling to my knees. I started crying hysterically, and that was my moment of truth. At that moment the awareness, or whatever you want to call it, came across me, that I either had to quit drinking or die, and at that point I didn't particularly care which. But it was my first true awakening that alcohol was definitely the problem in my life. Somewhere in that same moment I was given the strength and the knowledge to call an old friend and a former family member that I knew was in AA. This man came over and spent the evening talking with me. An important factor I like to remember about that night, Faith, is that through the whole evening while we were talking, and I'm in and out of a blackout, talking and crying, I wanted never to pick up a drink again, and yet I would have cut off my right arm for a drink at the same time. So the tug-of-war started right from that moment.

He asked me if I would go to a meeting with him the next evening, if I'd try to stay away from a drink for just that next day, the next twenty-four hours. I said I would try. He picked me up, and I went to my first AA meeting. I remember trying to look anonymous and not wanting anyone to come up and talk with me. I picked up what we call a schedule book and opened it. There's twenty questions in there to help you determine whether you might have a problem with alcohol. I went through the twenty questions and I was able to answer yes to nineteen out of the twenty. The meeting started, a meeting where there was a speaker and discussion around the table. When it came to me I was able to say that my name was Rob and I was an alcoholic, and oh, boy, did I choke on those words. That was not easy but at that moment it was like the weight of the world had lifted off my shoulders. It was a beautiful experience; I was given the gift of having a greater desire to stay sober than was my desire to drink. From that point to this, one day at a time, I dove into the program headfirst. Members of AA were really willing to help. Geez, I had people picking me up every night, calling me every day, taking me to meetings, making suggestions as to what I might do to stay sober. One day at a time, it started working. I remember I had a calendar in my kitchen and I started crossing the days off. At the end of the day, I'd get all the lights off, I'd run to the calendar, mark off the day, and jump in bed. I knew I was pretty safe there at least until morning. Days started adding up, and months started adding up, and the desire to drink started lifting more. People in the program helped get me involved in making coffee at meetings and doing various jobs. I'm grateful for AA. My life has turned around 180 degrees. One day at a time it will be twelve years on November twelfth.

JOY: I was listening to a woman who was having trouble with the God stuff, and I identified very strongly because when I first tried AA, that's very much the way that I felt. I did white-knuckle sobriety as a result of that for about a year. Actually, when I was finally convinced to go back to AA by someone, it was a friend who enthusiastically shared with me how her life had changed. I had made a comment, "Gosh, you've changed." And what I got back was a story about how participating in the fellowship of AA had changed her life. Early on I looked at God as standing for Group Of Drunks instead of having to have a spiritual or religious higher power. Now, several years later, I do have a higher power. As many people say, if you don't get it right away, it'll get you if you just keep on coming.

WHY GO TO MEETINGS IF YOU'RE SOBER?

LOUISE: When I first came into the program, I knew deep down inside that I had to go because it was the only place I felt that I fit in. Then something changed. As I got better, I discovered I enjoyed the meetings. If I'm in a good mood, I want to go and share it. If I'm down, I want to be around people who are going to bring me back up because I can't afford to wallow around in self-pity and depression.

EILEEN: It's important for me to go because I need to stay sober. I've been in AA since 1978, but I still am an alcoholic. I haven't had a drink and I don't think about drinking, but I know that if I stop going to meetings that I might forget what it was like when I was drinking. So there's this slogan in AA about keeping the memory green. When I sit at a meeting and I listen to a newcomer, it reminds me of what it was like when I was drinking. The other part of the AA preamble is about helping other alcoholics to achieve sobriety. People with a lot of sobriety are a powerful example; it was very inspiring to me when I first came around to meetings to see somebody who had even a few months of sobriety, let alone several years. I think it's important for people to know that you can become a happy, useful person without drinking. It's wonderful. The meetings, as years go on, become more and more enriching to me.

FAITH: As a person who is not in AA, I found it surprising when I heard someone in AA say what you just said, "I don't even think about drinking." It was once my impression that people in AA walked around tortured all the time by alcohol advertising and seeing other people drink.

BARBARA: AA is where I belong; I feel comfortable. In many other social situations, I do not feel comfortable. I try to keep the memory green of what it was like when alcohol had control of me instead of my having control of my own life. It's a strange thing to walk into an AA meeting and suddenly know that you belong, that you're someplace where it's home. That's why I keep going. It will be thirty-five years if I don't drink for the next five days.

ANDREA: I was told early on some things that helped me a lot. One was that going to an AA meeting was like putting money in the bank; if I went to meetings, I would have a lot to fall back on, when I had a problem. That's really been true for me. Every time I go to a meeting, I feel a little bit richer. The other thing I was told that was helpful was that there were two times to go to a meeting —when I wanted to and when I didn't, and if I would go those two times, I would stay sober. That has turned out to be true. When I got to be around ten years sober, I really felt that I wanted to graduate. I wanted to go to AA out of the largeness of my heart, to spread some wisdom. I wanted to look back from my lofty place at the mess I had made when I was an alcoholic. Two things started to happen. One is that eventually I cut way back on my meetings and I didn't talk in meetings the same

way about what was going on with me. I started wanting
to drink. There was nothing wrong in my life, but that
voice started that said, "Oh you're so sober now. You're
so healthy. You could have a drink like a normal person."
For me to consider having a drink is insane. For someone
to have happen to them what happened to me from
drinking, and to ever consider it again, that's already my
alcoholism talking. The other thing is that my thinking
goes out of whack if I don't go to meetings. Wires start
hanging out of my head; we get Mr. Hyde instead of Dr.
Jekyll.

NORM: If I miss meetings, if something goes on or I've
been sick, I get out of whack. We were talking the other
day about when our kids were all home; they used to line
up and vote and say, "Yes, Dad, you need to go to meetings." It says in the AA Big Book that we're not cured of
alcoholism. What we really have is a daily reprieve based
upon the maintenance of our spiritual condition. That's
why we keep talking about a day at a time. We need to
keep going to meetings to maintain our spiritual condition.

FAITH: What do people in AA mean by "spiritual"?

EILEEN: It's not religious. There are many different
kinds of people in AA. There are people who are quite
religious and belong to denominations and go regularly
to church or synagogue, and then there are people who
don't. I think it's interesting when you look at the steps
of AA and you see, for example, Step Three is that we
turn our lives and will over to the care of God as we

understand him. That's underlined, because it's a very personal, intimate thing. My relationship with my higher power is completely different, I would suspect, from Norman's or Andrea's.

BARBARA: I've been listening to so many serious people here today, I forget that half of the program is just laughing and enjoying ourselves and having a good time. There's always someone who comes up with some crazy remarks. In response to your question, Faith, about the spiritual part of the program, I've heard it said that religion is for people who don't want to go to hell, and spirituality is for people who've been there.

Trust Radio

1

The following letter, addressed to me, was written anonymously and had a smiley face pasted on it:

Get out of the studio, far far away from the pseudo superficial people and events that now characterize your increasingly boring, pathetic shows. Go among the whores, the sluts, the drug addicts, the murderers, rapists, illiterates, dirty, weird, bizarre, etc., etc. Run to them and you will again become alive. Run! Run! Run!

—Rhode Island

Another letter was written in black Magic Marker on yellow lined school notebook paper:

Congratulations, oh mighty ones! Still you manage to consistently produce some of the worse public radio programming in the nation; indeed, in the entire world. And the absolute jewel of your dismal programs is the daily 4–5 superficial "girlie show," such shallowness is for sure unmatched anywhere!

Many people have asked why I think there is such interest in aggression. Philosopher Ram Dass told me in an interview that possibly our attention is captured by aggression because we get an adrenaline hit from it that goodness does not provide. My own view is that to specialists in the politics of demonization, goodness and its reporters are frequently fair game. If offering an atmosphere that respects subtlety and heart rather than extremism and hate opens me to the charge of sentimentality, I'll take the risk. I like what the writer Gail Godwin said when asked why she feels the need to modulate suffering with sweet reasonableness and humor. She said, Honey, that's what they call character. I believe that there is no better way to build fine character than to recognize it wherever it exists. Listening for goodness and noticing achievement can make all the difference in the world.

At a speech one evening, someone asked why I seek stories about our humanity. These stories inspire me, and I believe that they are important. I suspect that a fair number of my colleagues would agree. Most reporters I know are decent people who face and must handle real marketplace pressures. Nevertheless, there are questions about goodness that are worth considering: Is goodness deep, or is it intellectually shabby? If criticism is an art, should the recognition of achievement be one, too? Why does an interest in goodness suggest we are unrealistic?

Can we separate sentiment from sentimentality? Can we commit to investigating goodness and not give up on exposing what is wrong? Do we know how to make stories of goodness and the qualities that give us our humanity as interesting as stories about tragedy and scandal?

2

It was Aristotle who said that conflict is the essence of drama. True, failure is an interesting and worthy subject.

Like most Americans, I settle in each night to watch the local and national TV news. I see video of a man swept into rushing floodwaters near his home, grasping for a rescuer's hand before being pulled under to his death; I read stories of babies left in Dumpsters, of a man set on fire because he is African American. I think we have become like the characters in *The Lord of the Flies,* and I am momentarily convinced of our total preoccupation with violence, our lack of concern for one another, our ignorance and intolerance. And I begin to believe newspaper stories that say we are a rootless society, incapable of acting like true neighbors, and uninterested even in living near our own aging relatives. But this view is askew, and I always come back to balance. I find myself in the unique position of having fifteen years of documentation of what psychologist Daniel Goleman refers to as emotional intelligence. My life is awash with people who interrupt their lives to call from phone booths or from their cars, who listen to the stories of others and are moved by them, who offer their tenderness and listening with no expectation of return. This is drive-by journalism of a different sort, this is trust radio, the secret voices of common goodness.

Working as I do and hearing what I hear has restored my faith in who we are. If faith is a belief in the unseen, the world is filled with people who take care of themselves and others, who live with insight and gratitude, who have fun, who understand a simple gesture, who know what being a good neighbor means, who care about injustice, who make mistakes and try to right them, who know how to live with differences, who commit themselves to being part of what is good. These are real people, and they are your neighbors as much as mine.

If this book has helped you remember an important story of your own, send it to me in care of the Stony Creek Post Office, Thimble Island Road, Branford, Connecticut 06405. Be sure to include your postal and/or e-mail address, and your telephone number.